and
now they
know.

Steidl

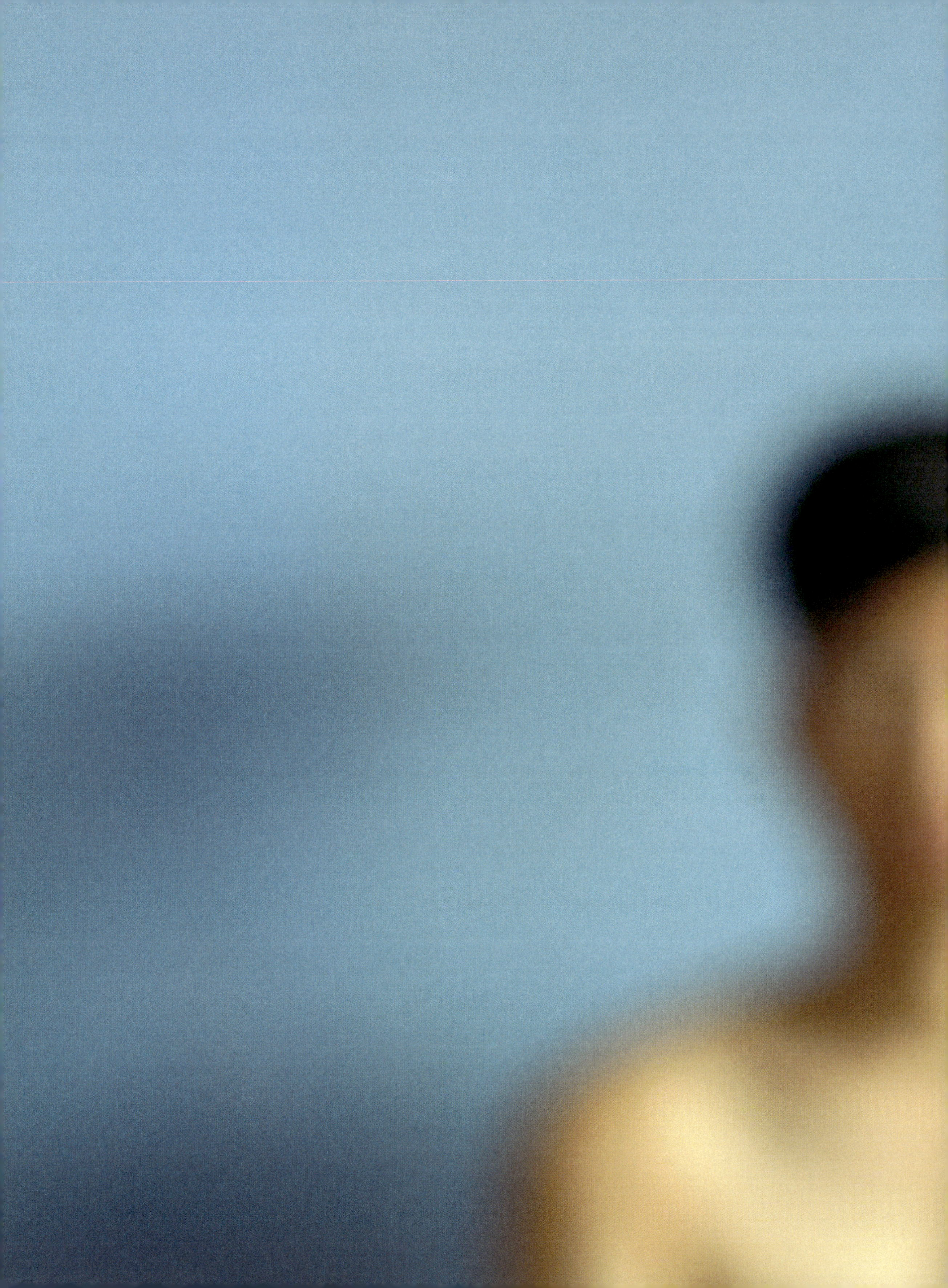

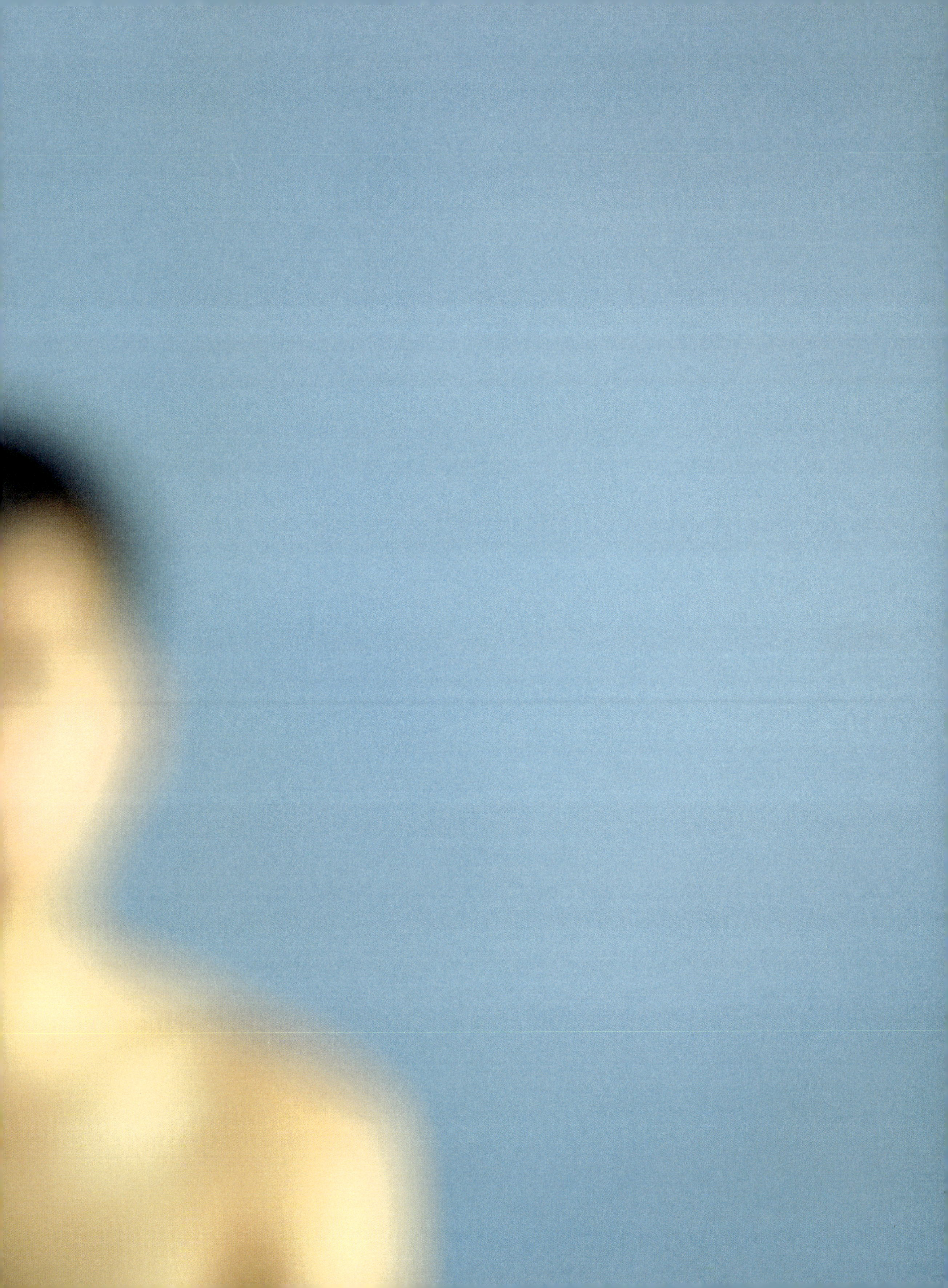

As I free fall
down the well of
my immature choices,
my skin peels,
disintegrating into
what remains of my reality.

As I hit the ground,
I shatter.
My truth has always been
an untouchable, unspeakable illusion.
I yearn for the wind to pick me.

Pick me.
Let me fly free.

When will I be free?
When will I be me?

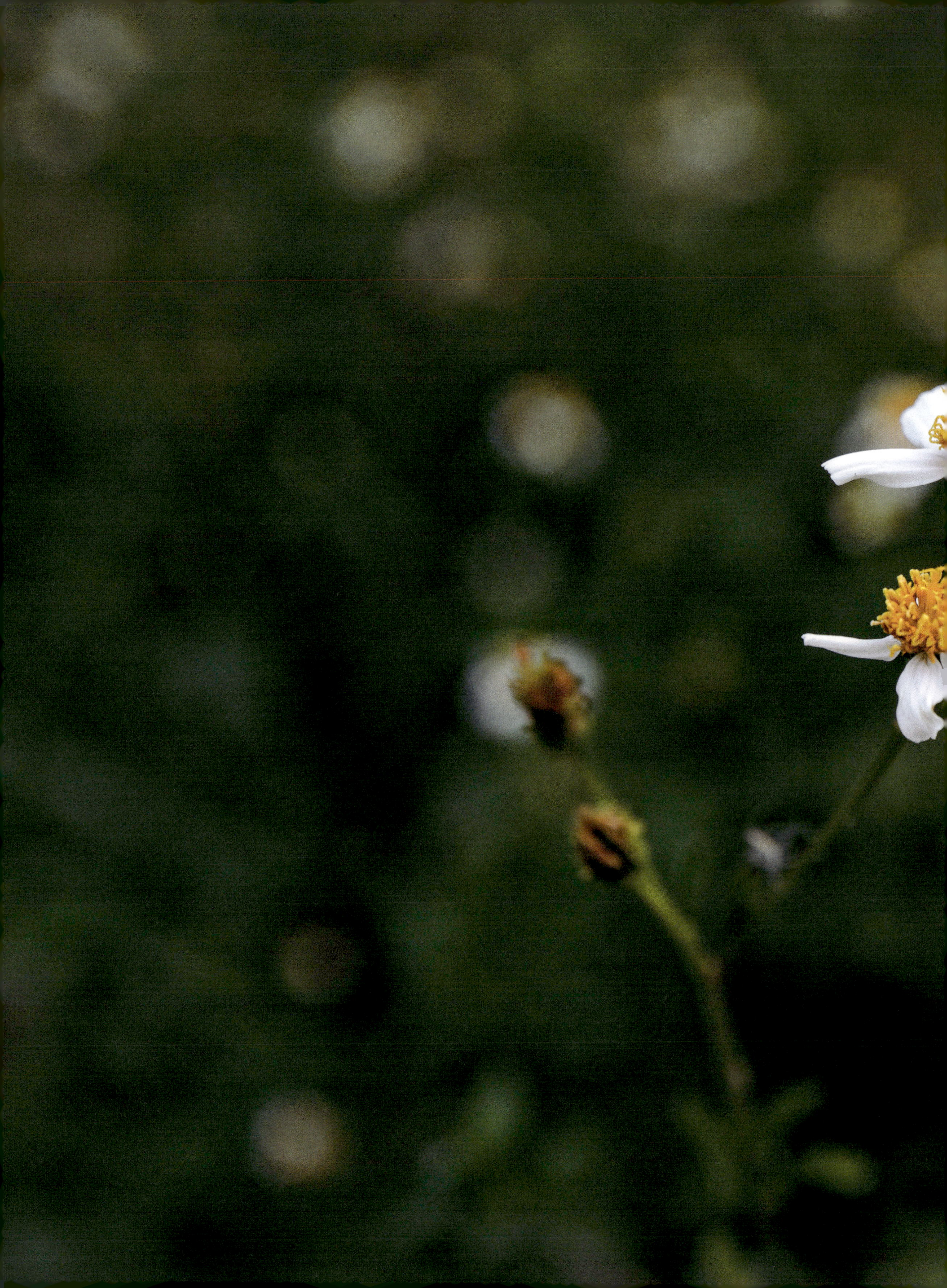

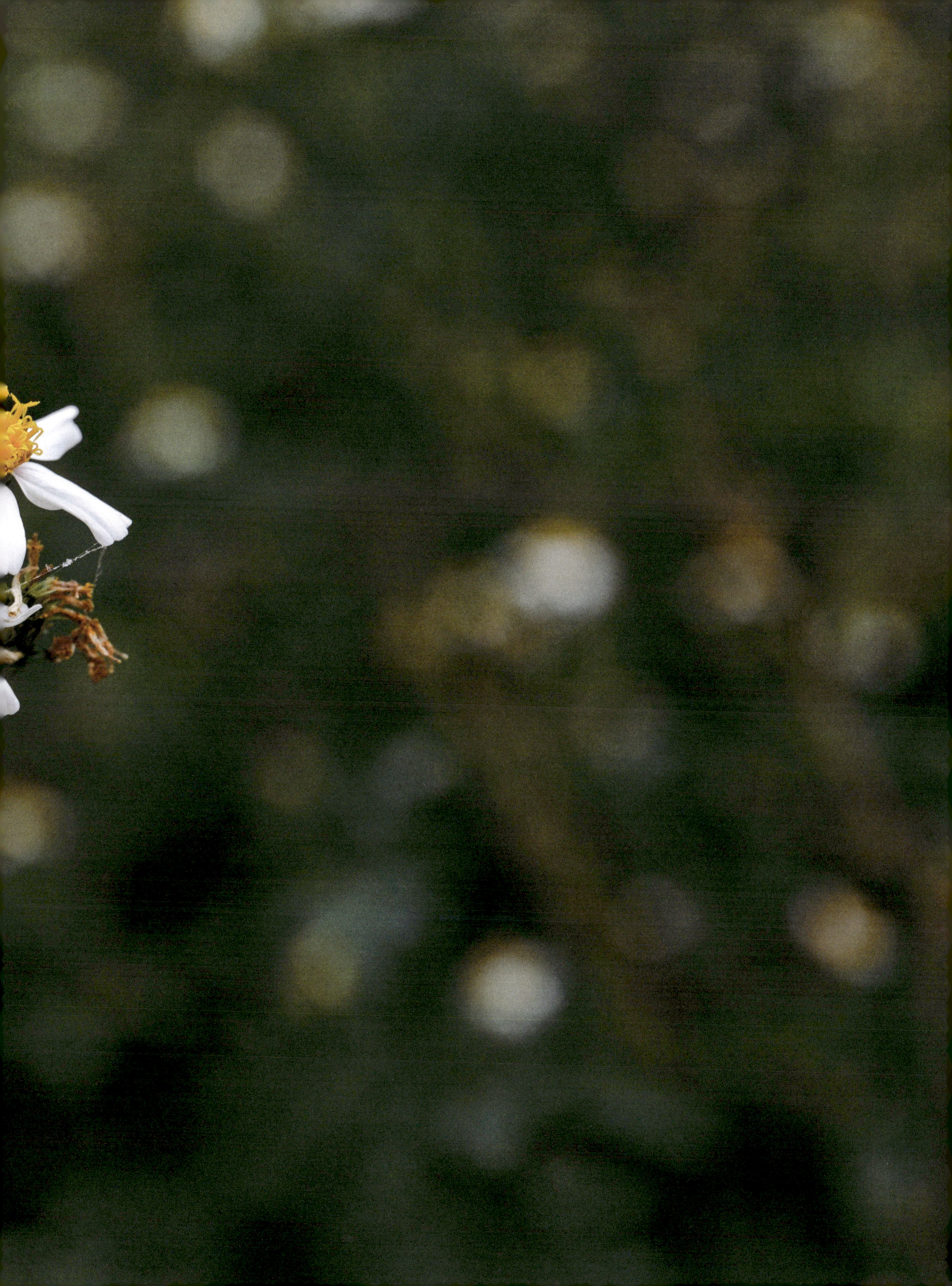

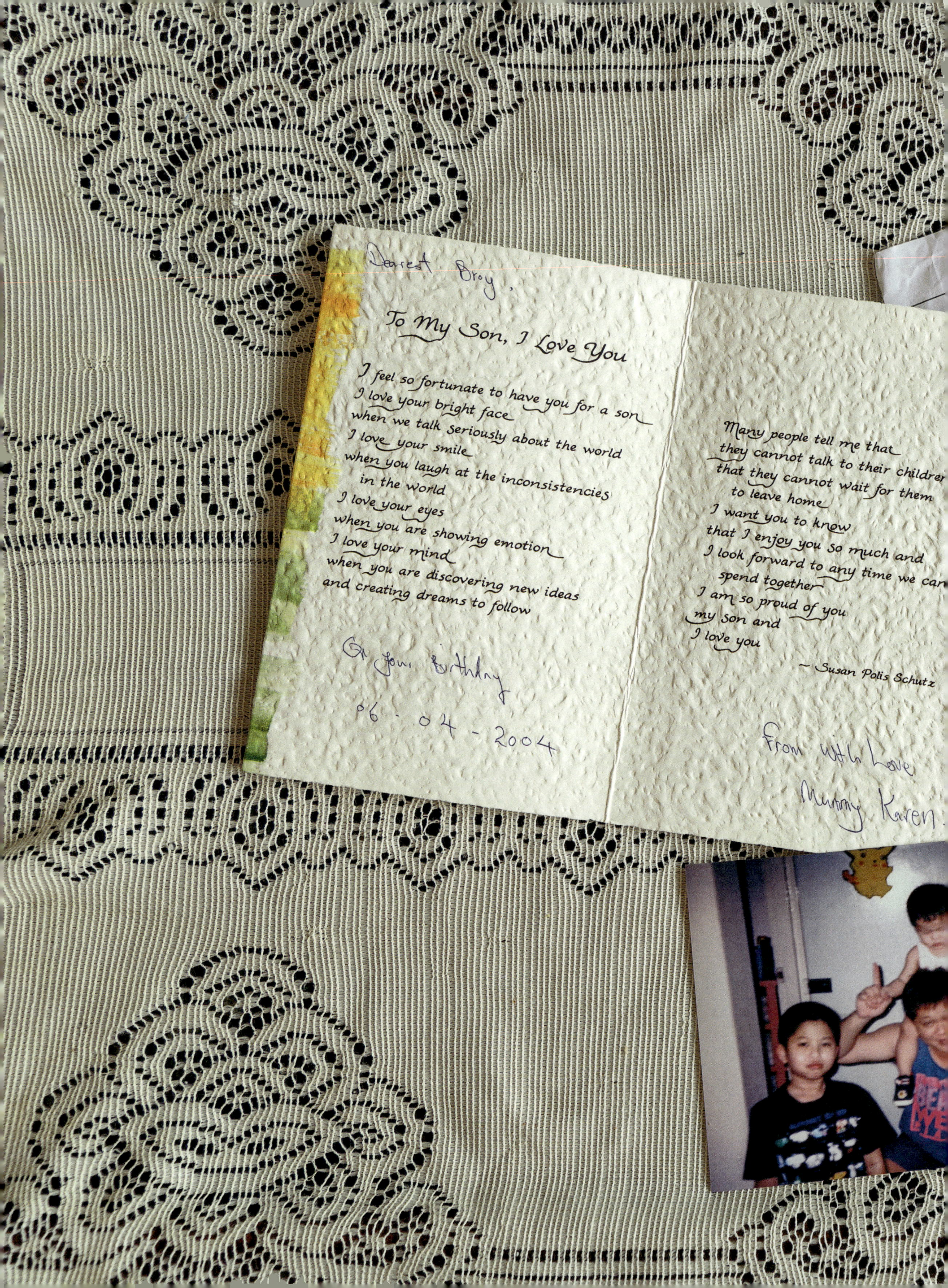
Dearest Broy,

To My Son, I Love You

I feel so fortunate to have you for a son
I love your bright face
when we talk seriously about the world
I love your smile
when you laugh at the inconsistencies
in the world
I love your eyes
when you are showing emotion
I love your mind
when you are discovering new ideas
and creating dreams to follow

On your Birthday
06 - 04 - 2004

Many people tell me that
they cannot talk to their children
that they cannot wait for them
to leave home
I want you to know
that I enjoy you so much and
I look forward to any time we can
spend together
I am so proud of you
my son and
I love you
— Susan Polis Schutz

From With Love
Mummy Karen

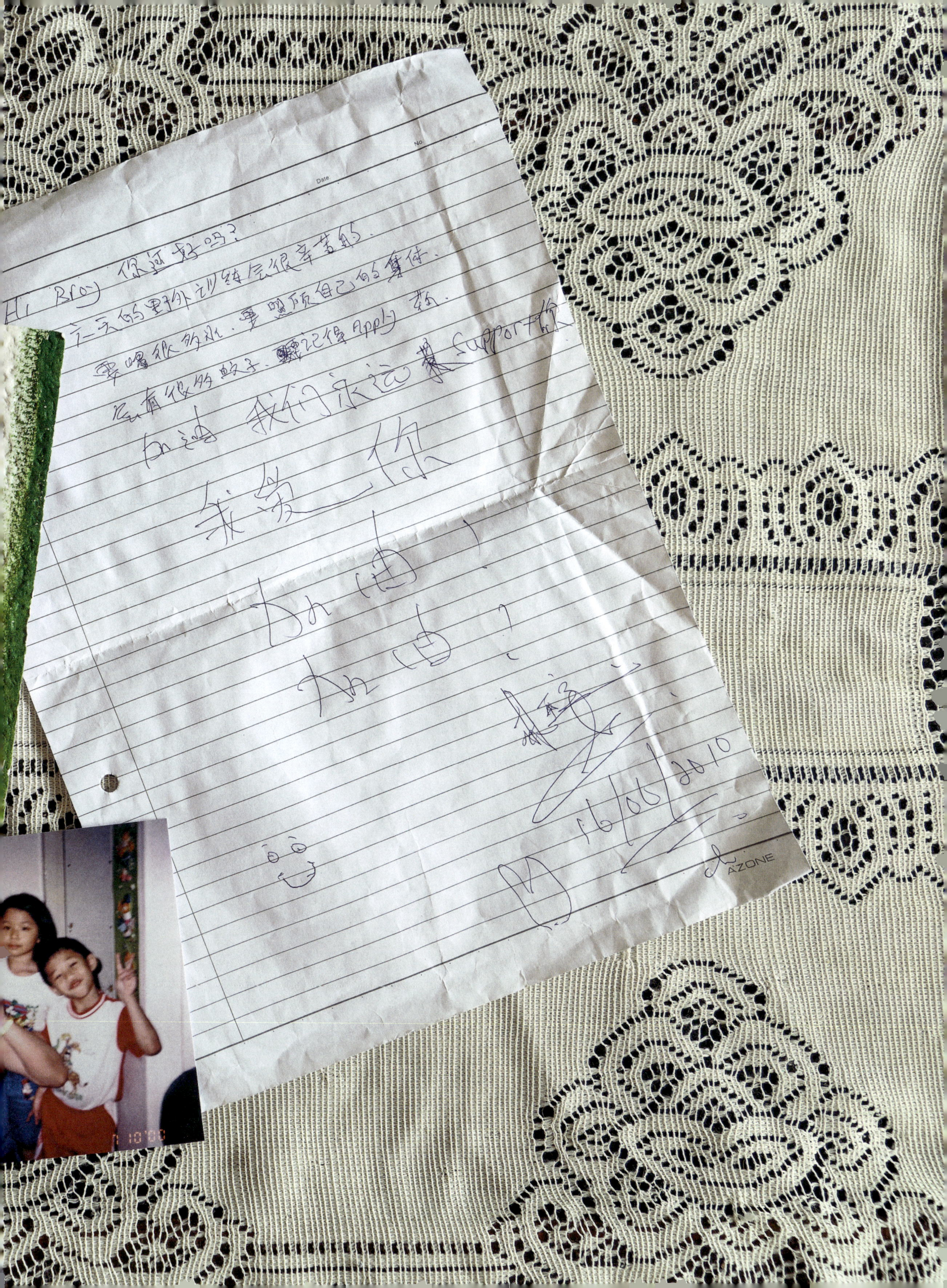

Hi Bro) 你过好吗?
三天的里外沙练忘很辛苦的.
要喝很多水. 要照顾自己的身体.
还有很多蚊子. 要记得 Apply 药.
加油 我们永远来 Support 你
我爱你
加油!
加油!
16/06/2010

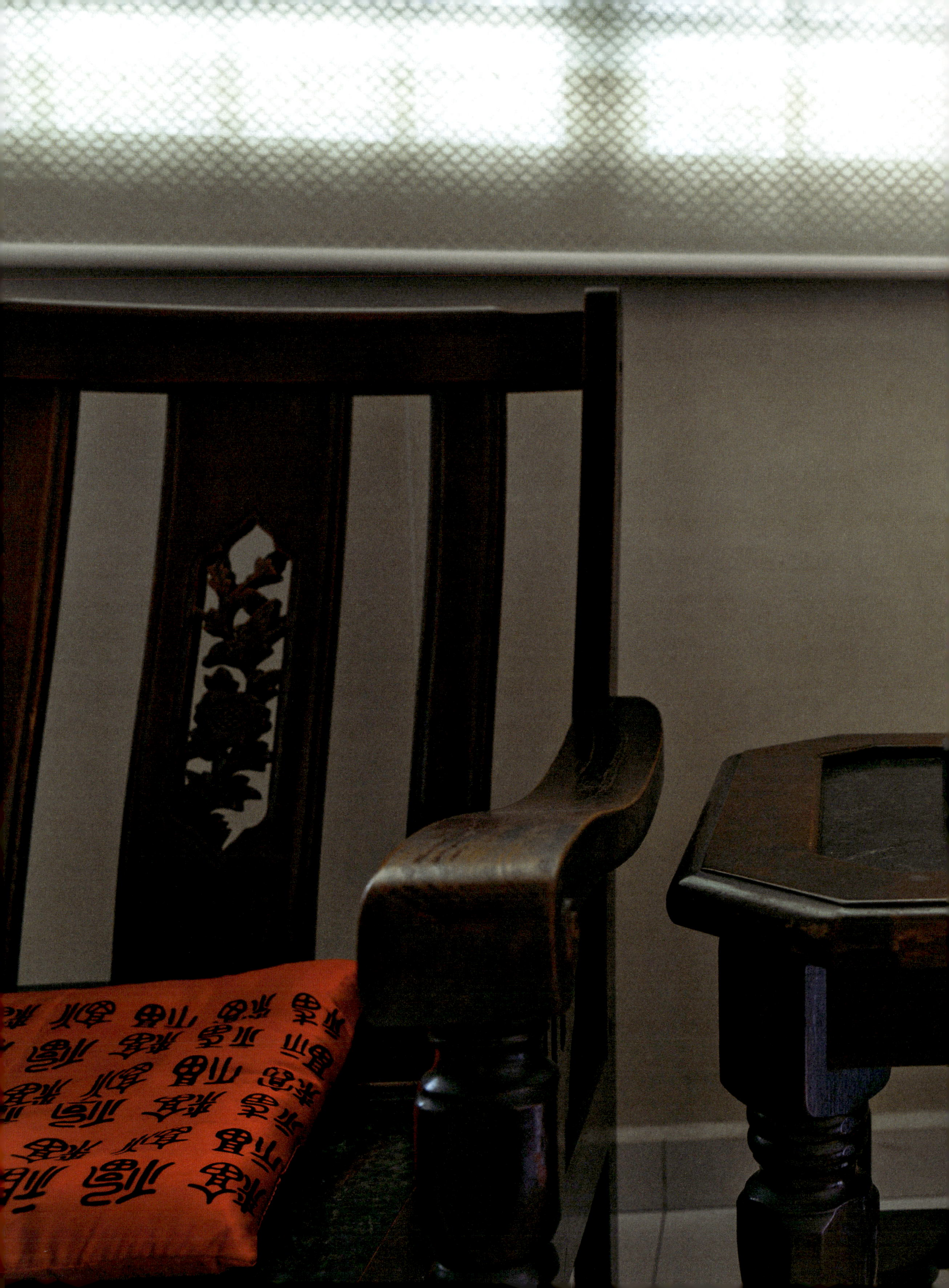

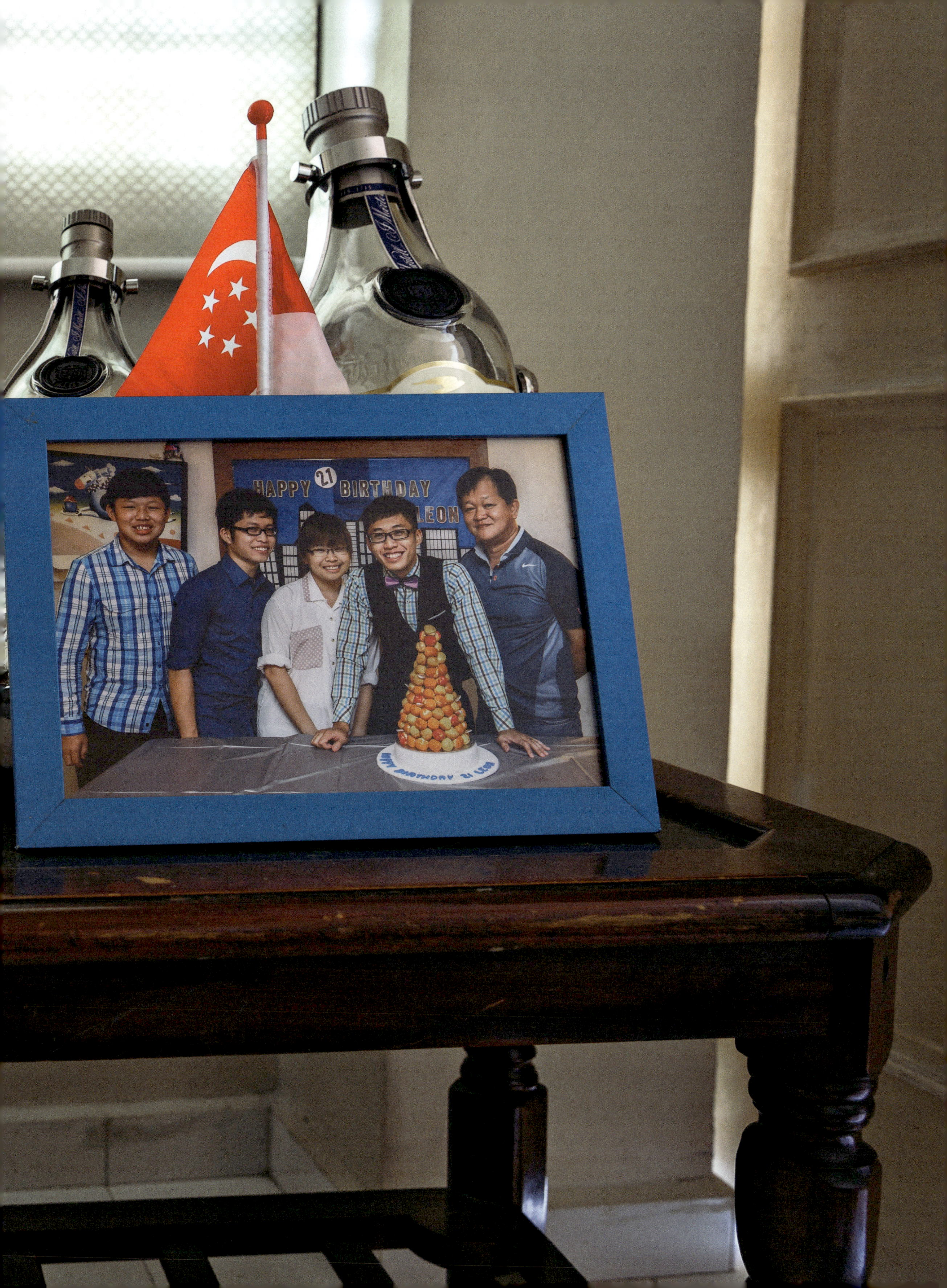

HAPPY 21 BIRTHDAY
LEON
HAPPY BIRTHDAY 21 LEON

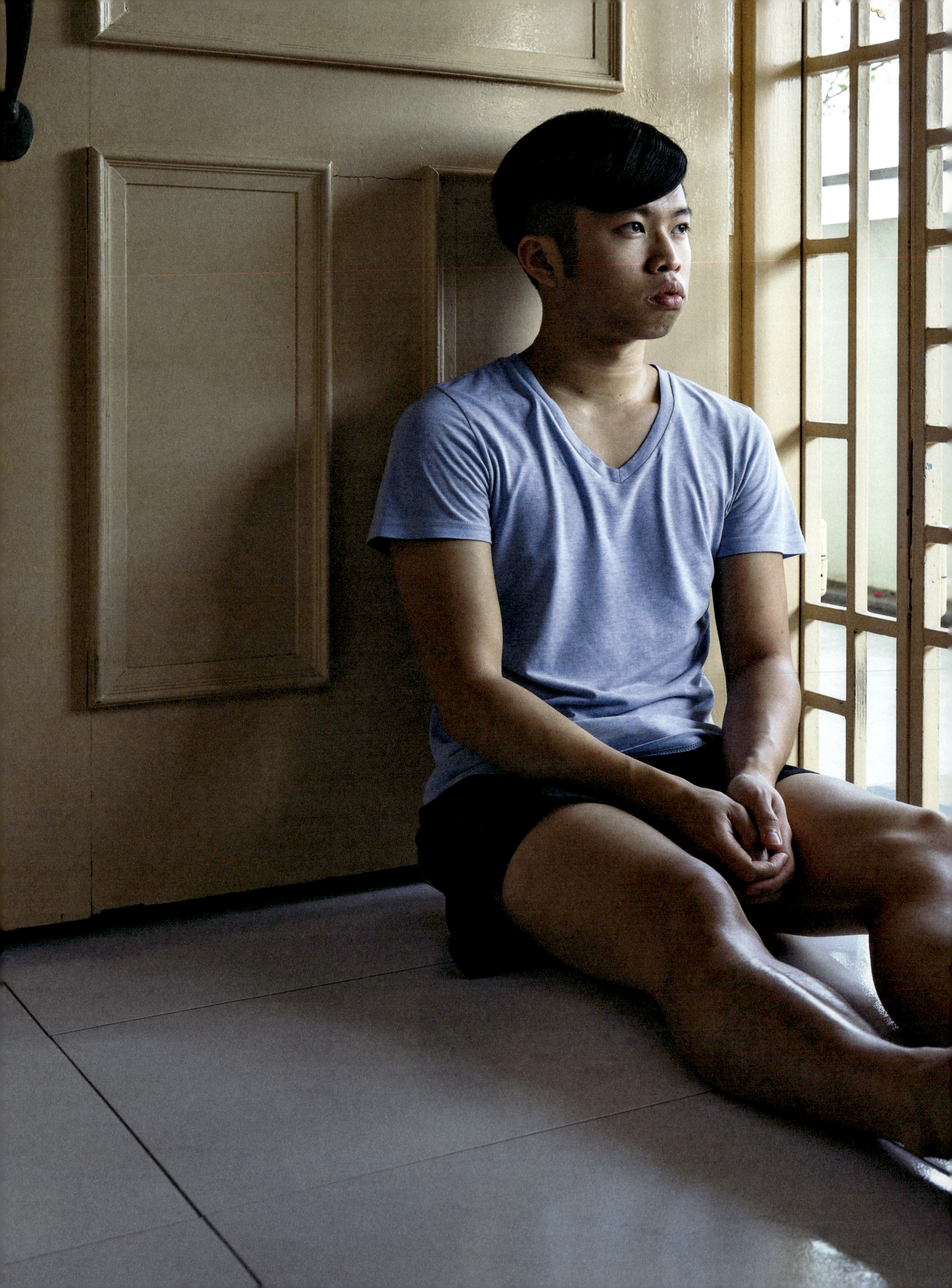

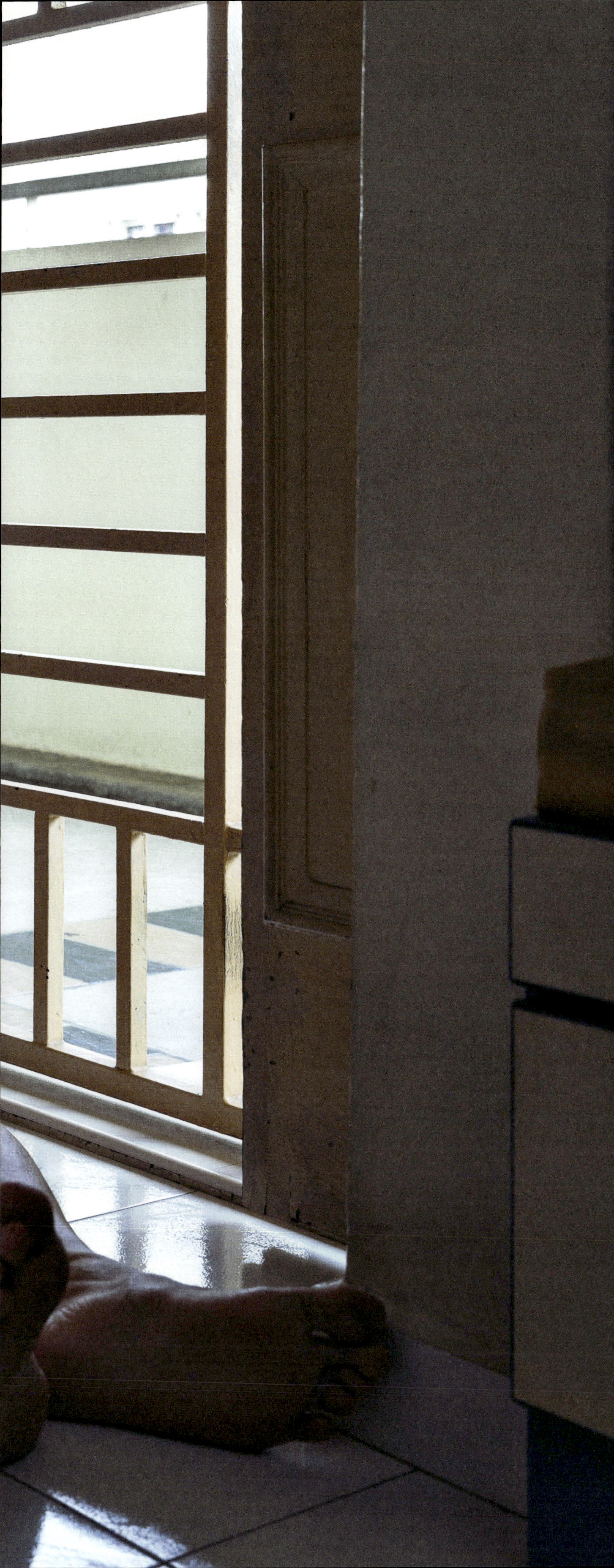

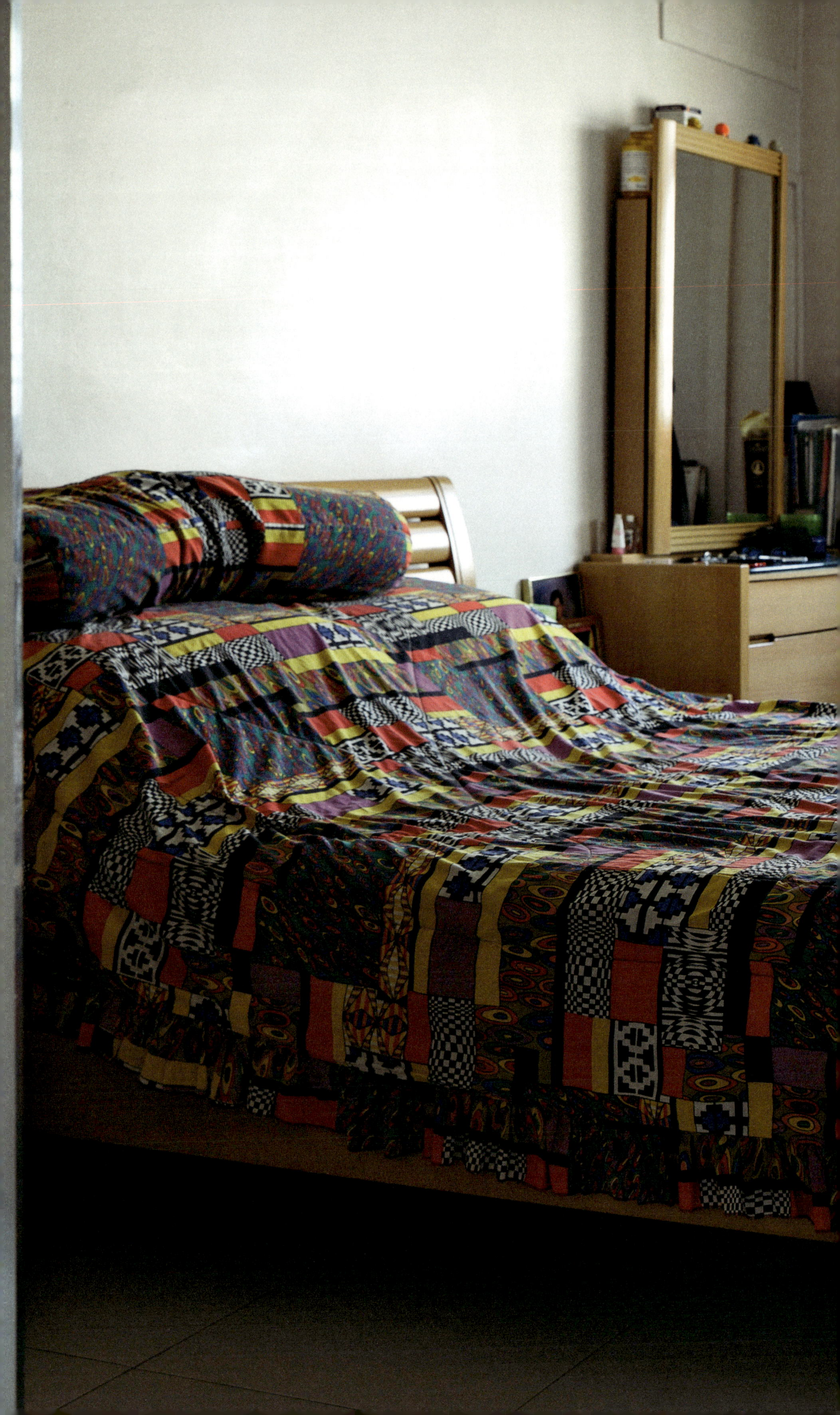

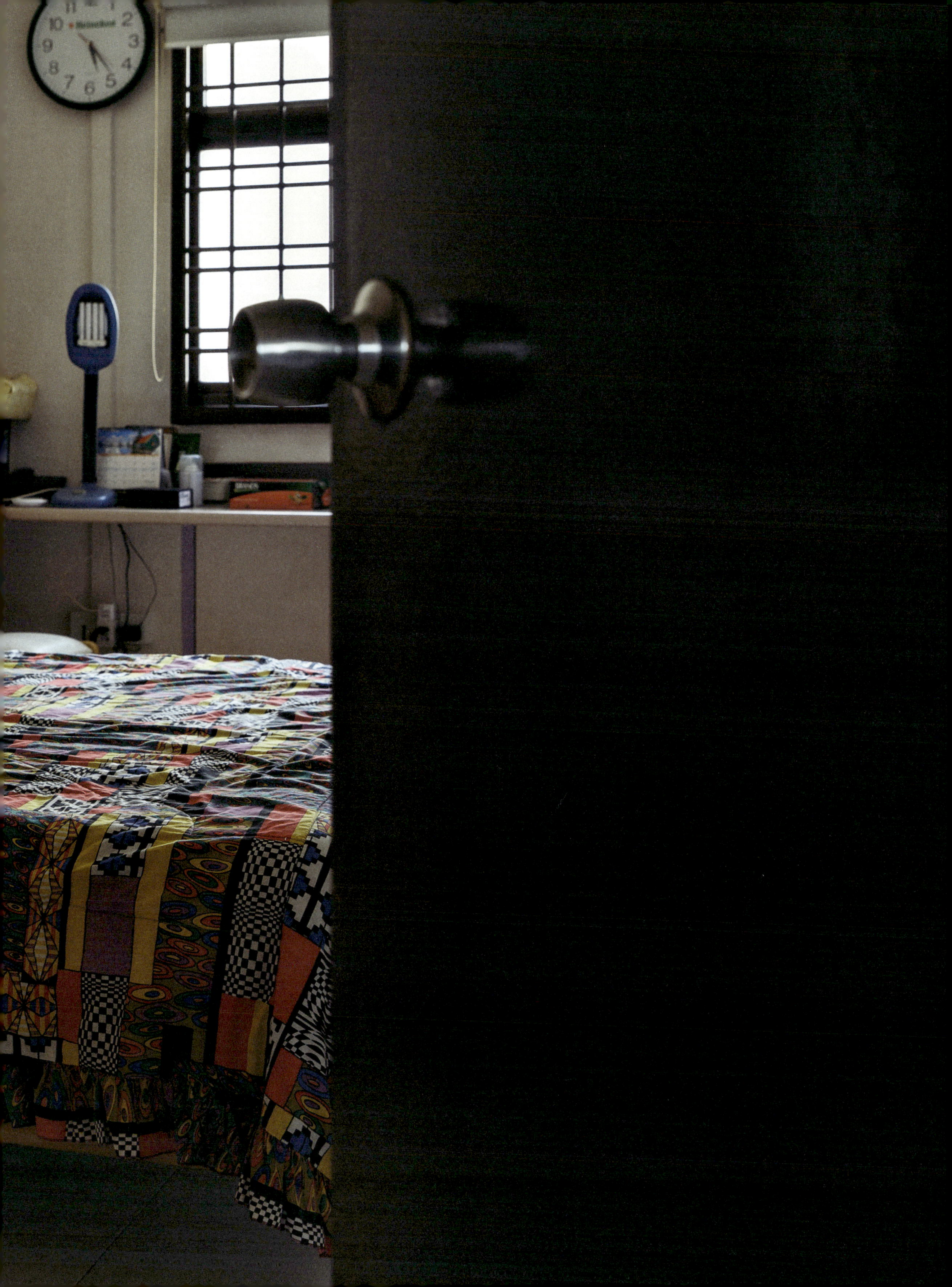

Unlimited, just like the star that you've became. I want to be unlimited too. So many times, I want to ascend to your paradise, to escape this inferno. I really want to but you would disapprove, wouldn't you? Yes, it's not time yet. We will meet again, on happier terms. If I burn, I will burn like your radiant, limitless light. Watch me burn, mummy. Watch me burn.

Don't speak. Don't make a sound. I know
you can see the lie I'm living. Even if
your silent approval or nonchalance were a
lie, let me indulge in this secret. And
pretend that you will let me be. Don't ask,
please daddy. Just let me be. Let us live
in our make-believes. Happily ever after.

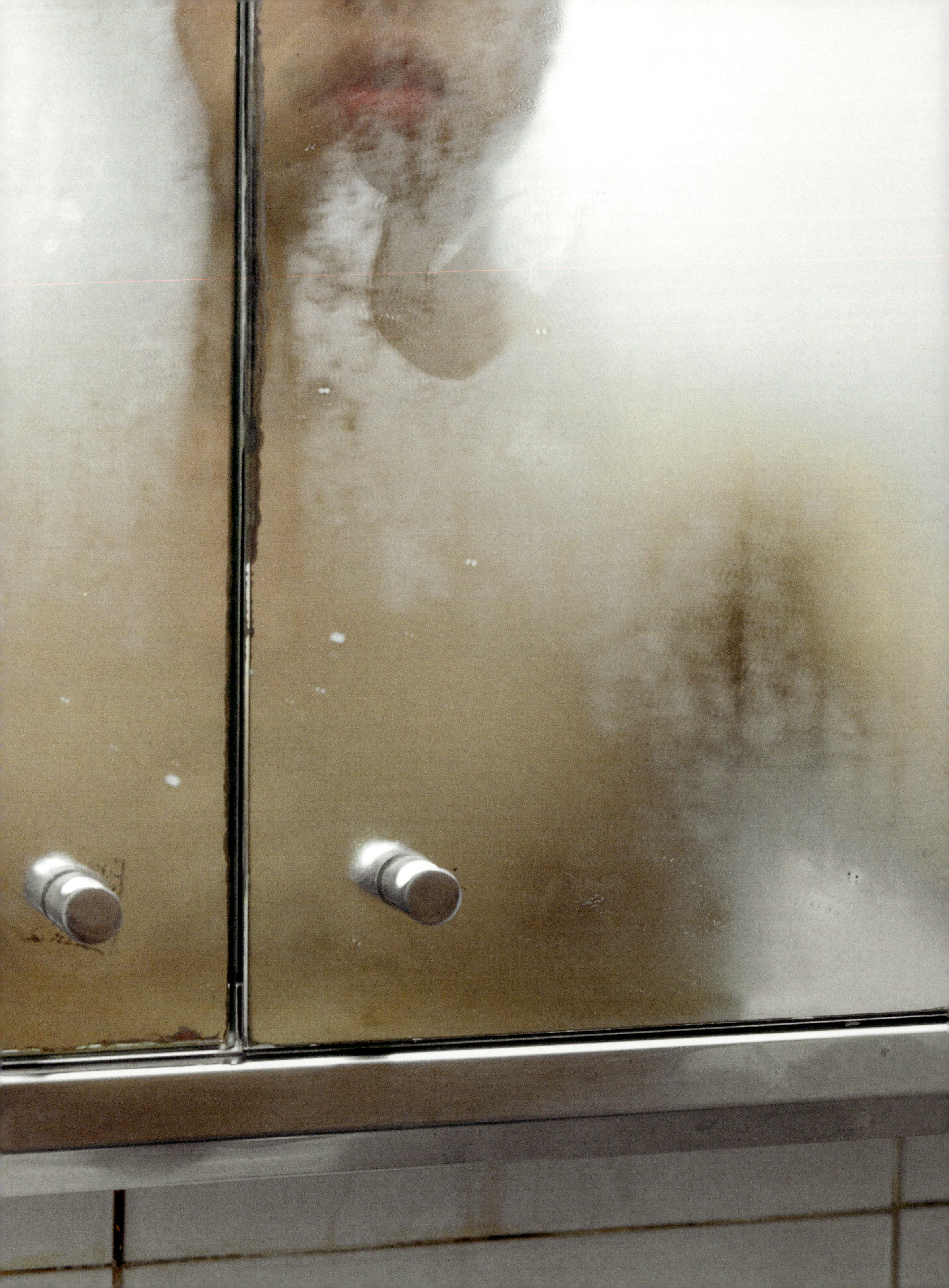

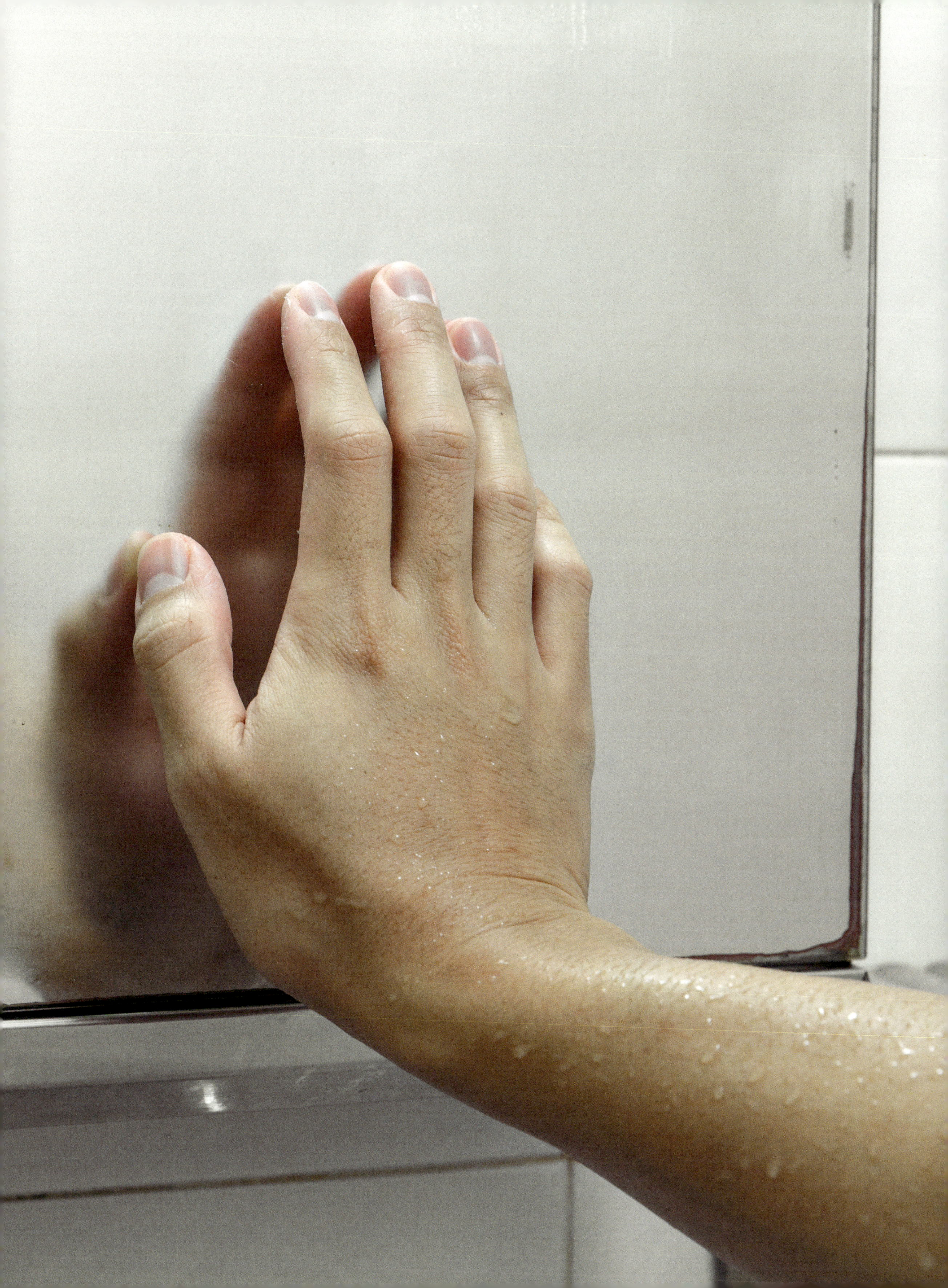

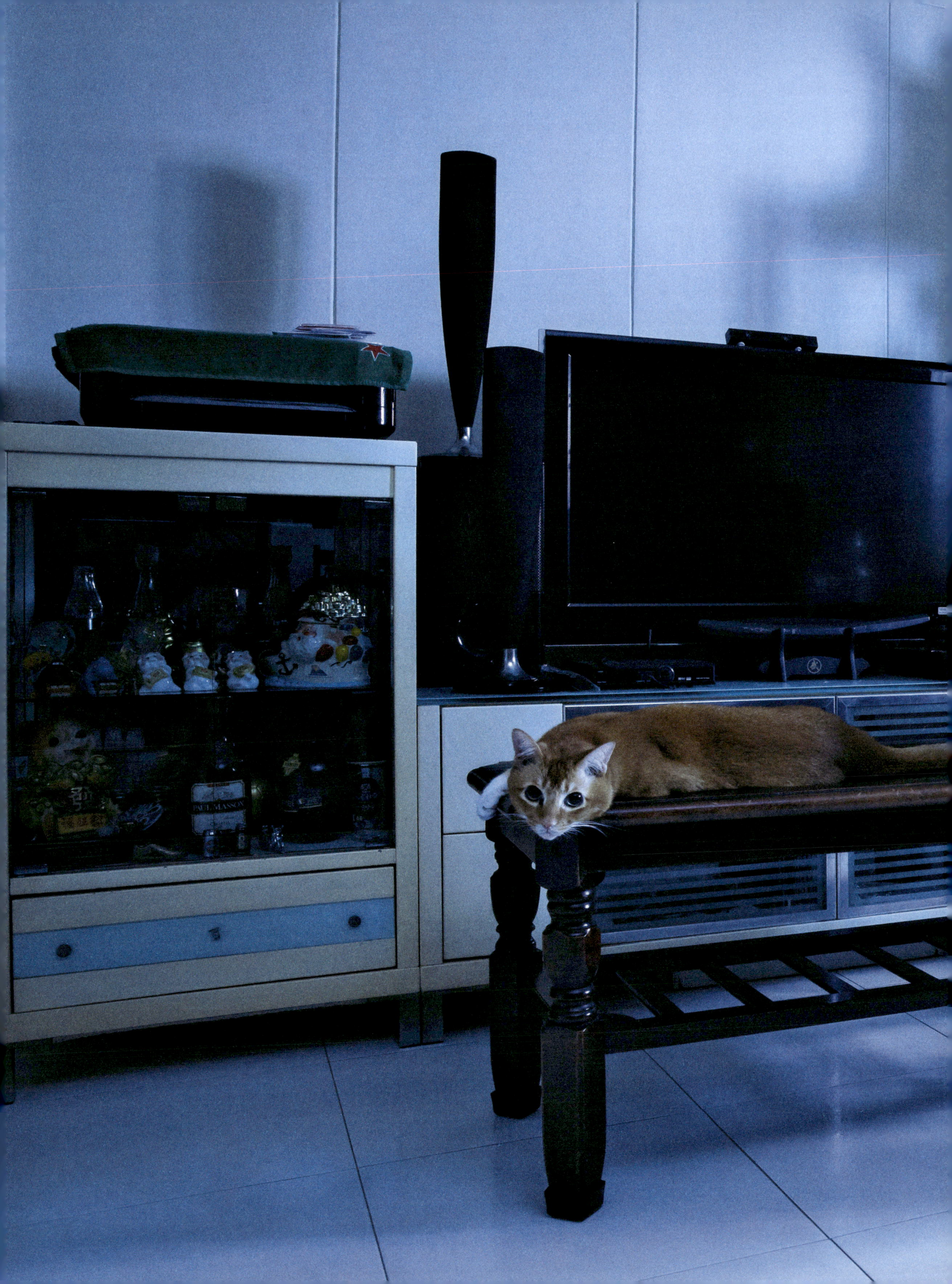

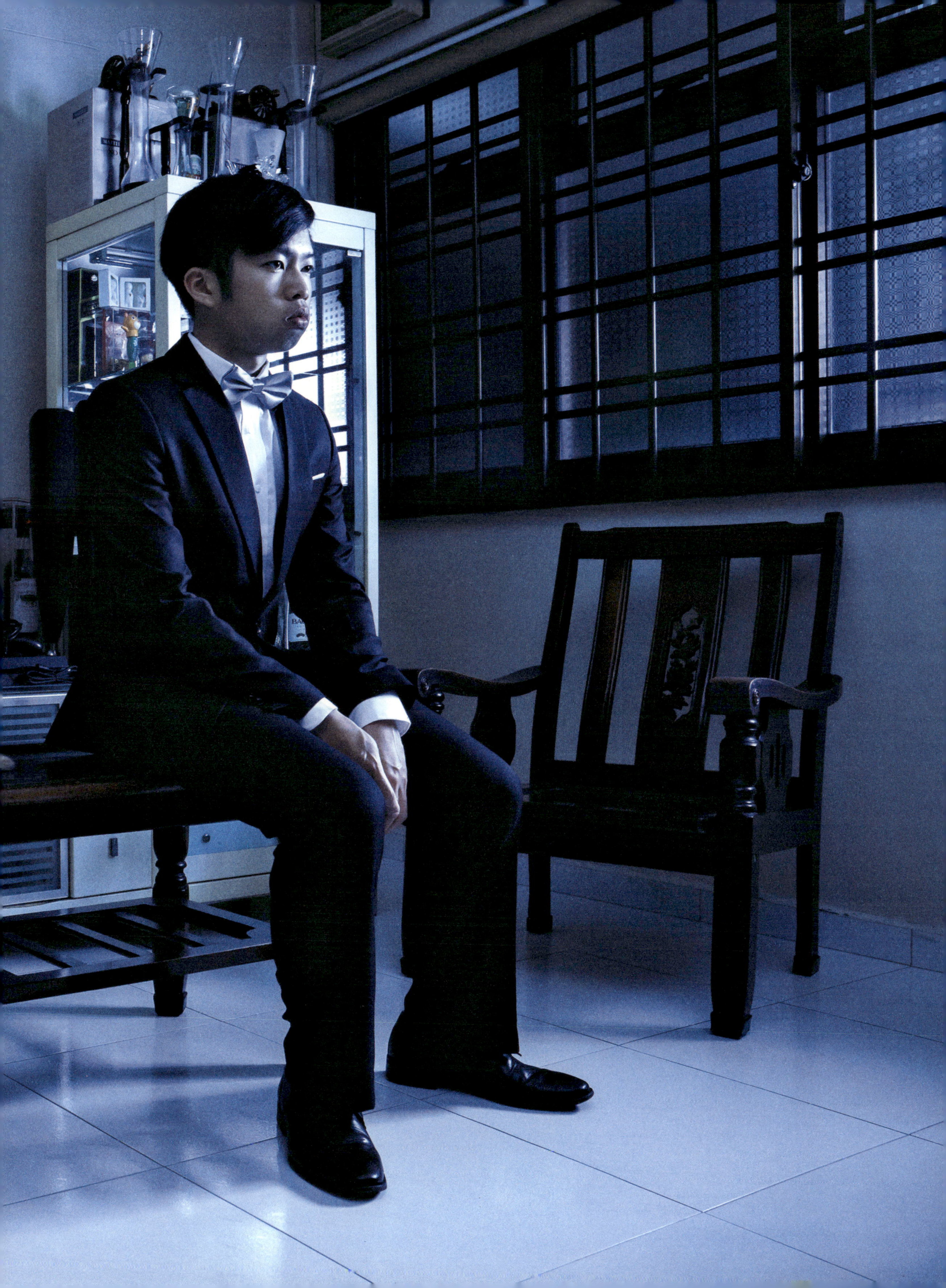

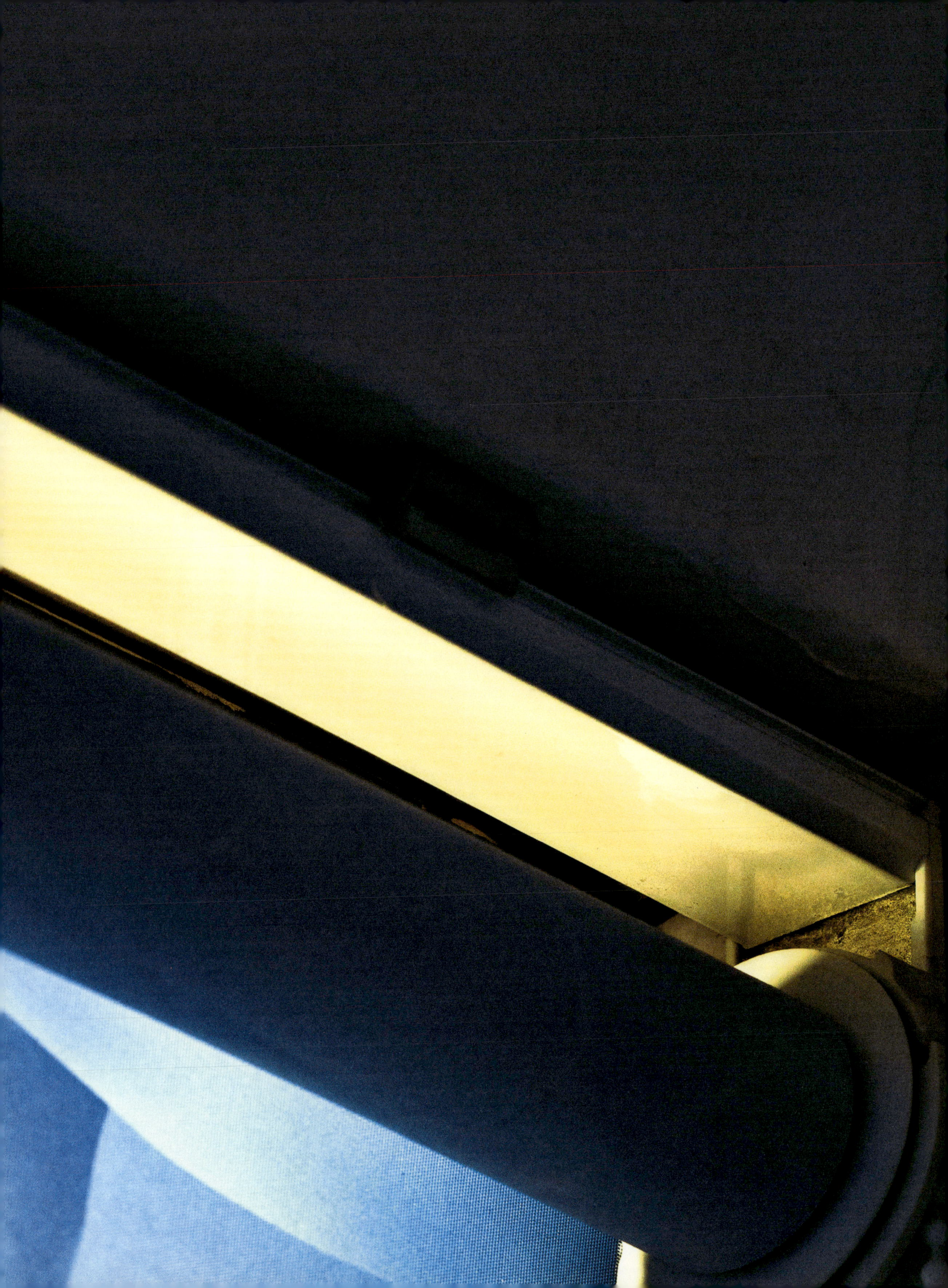

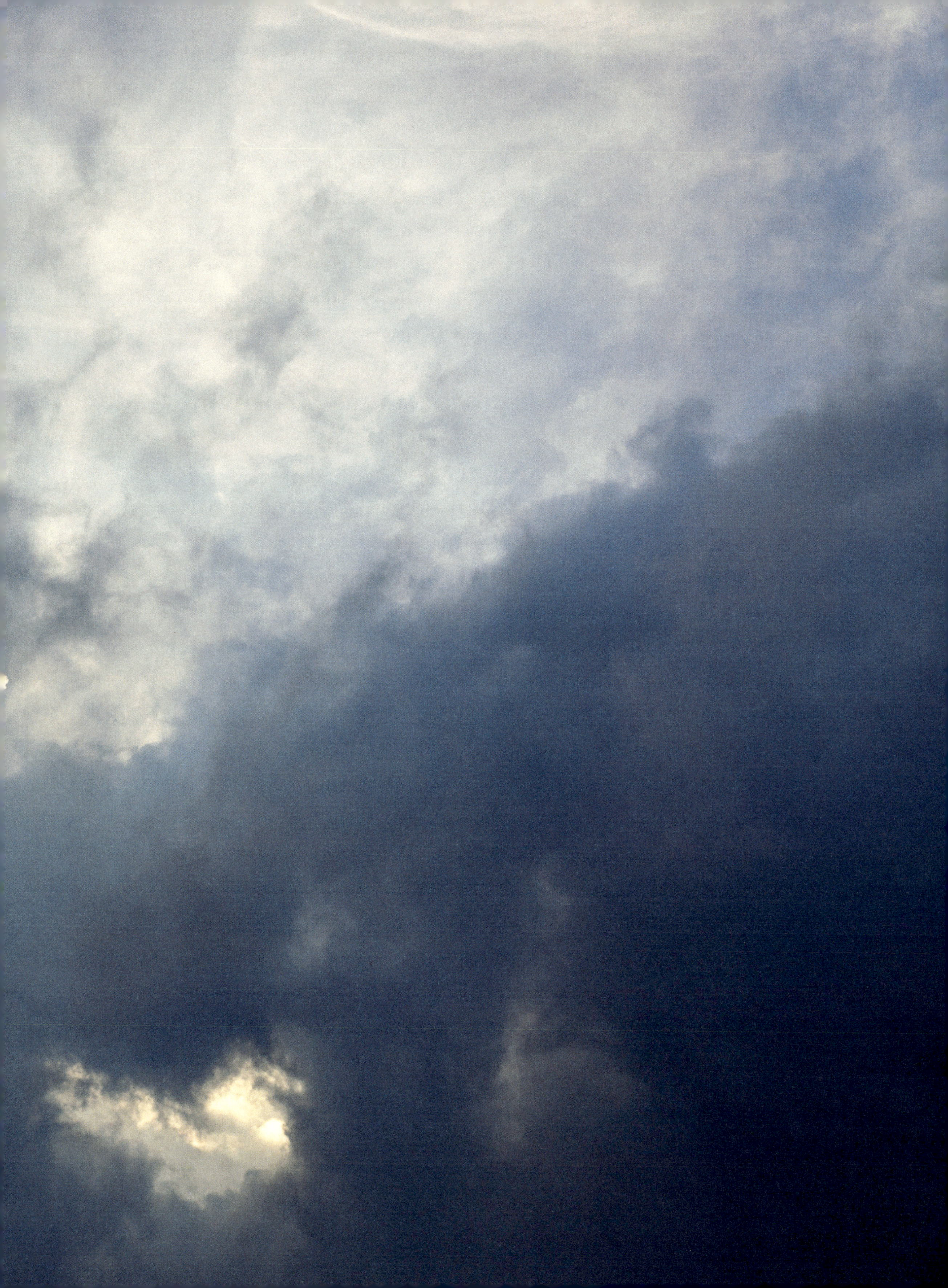

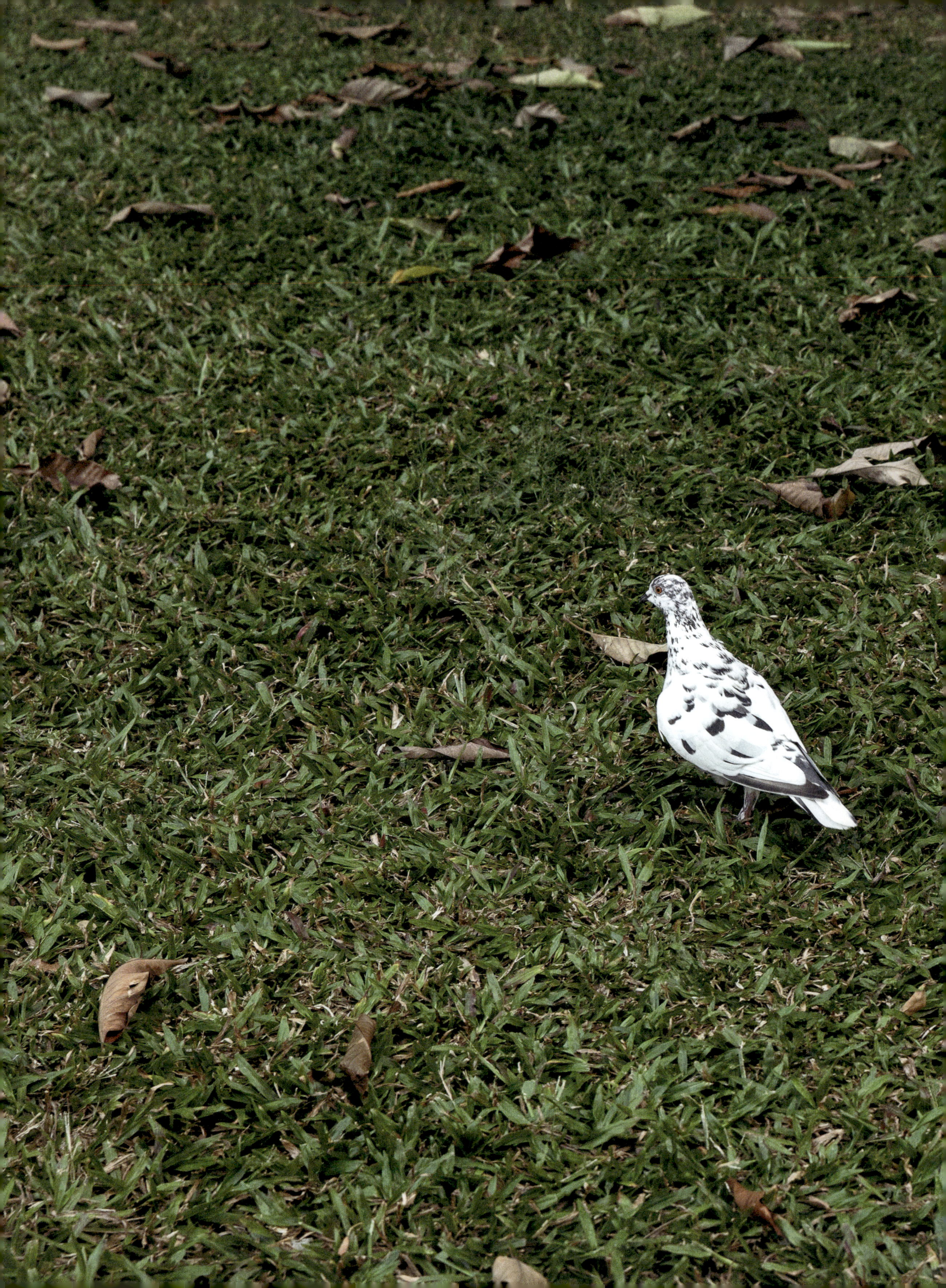

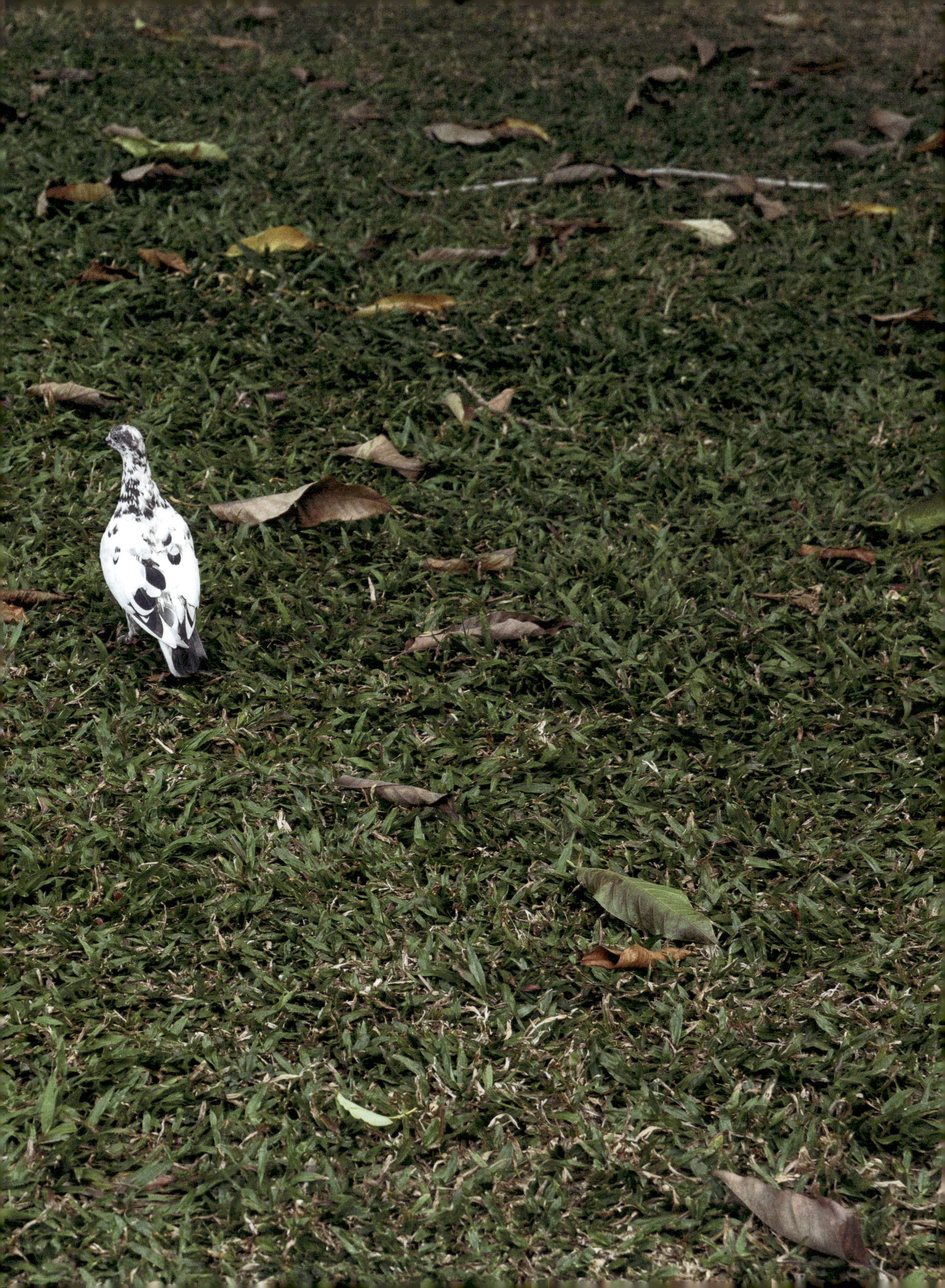

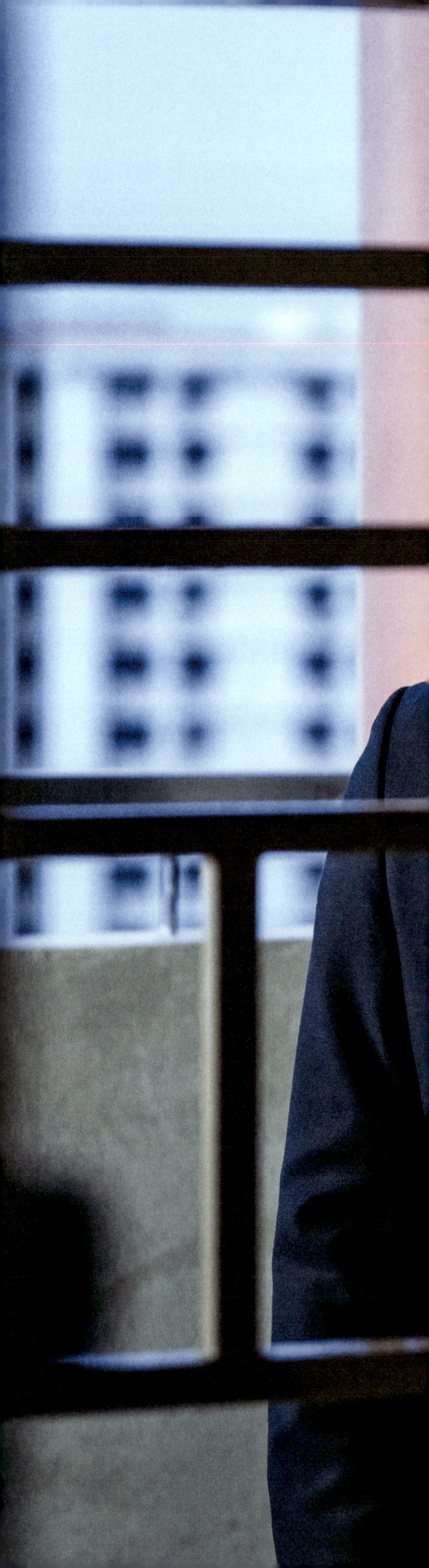

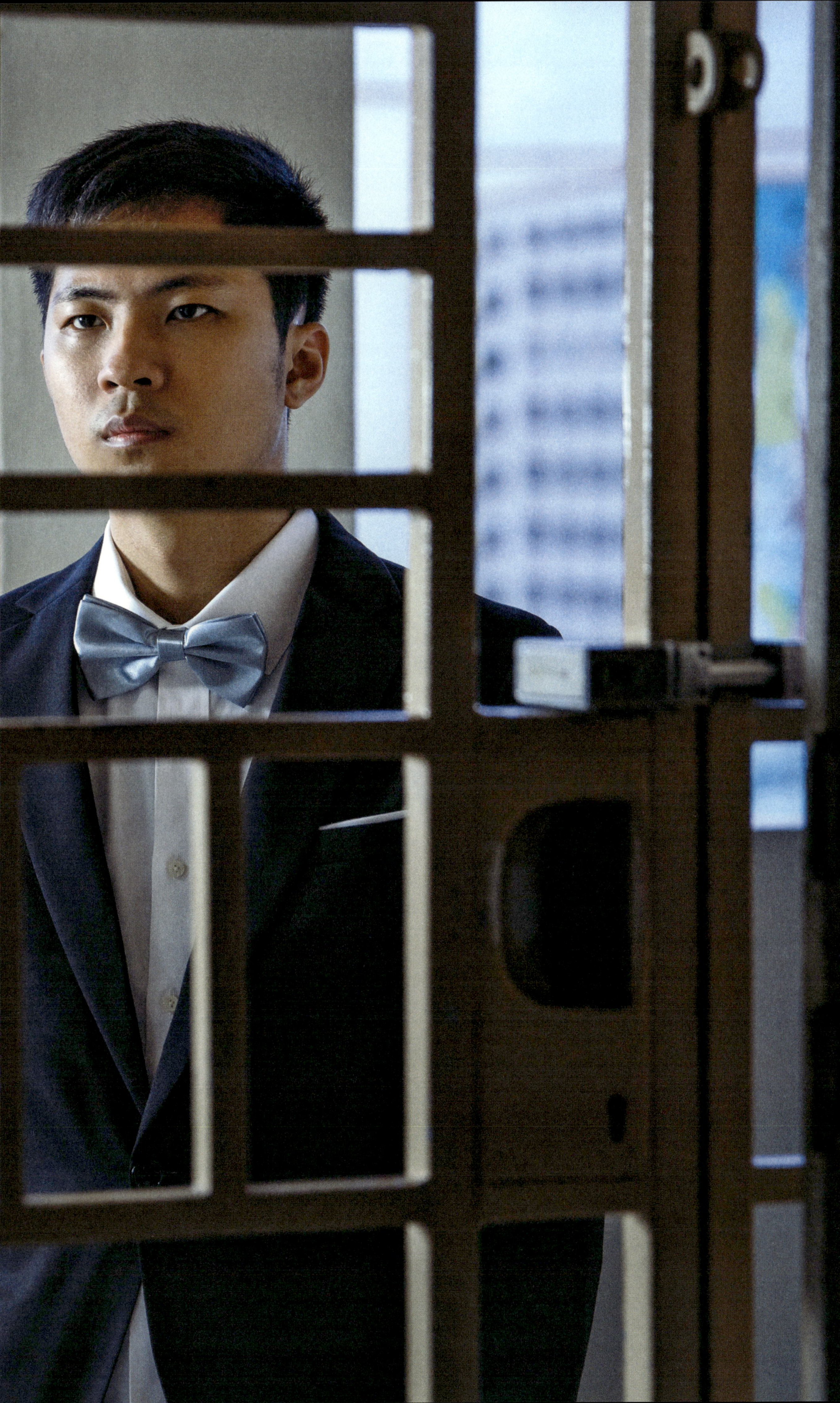

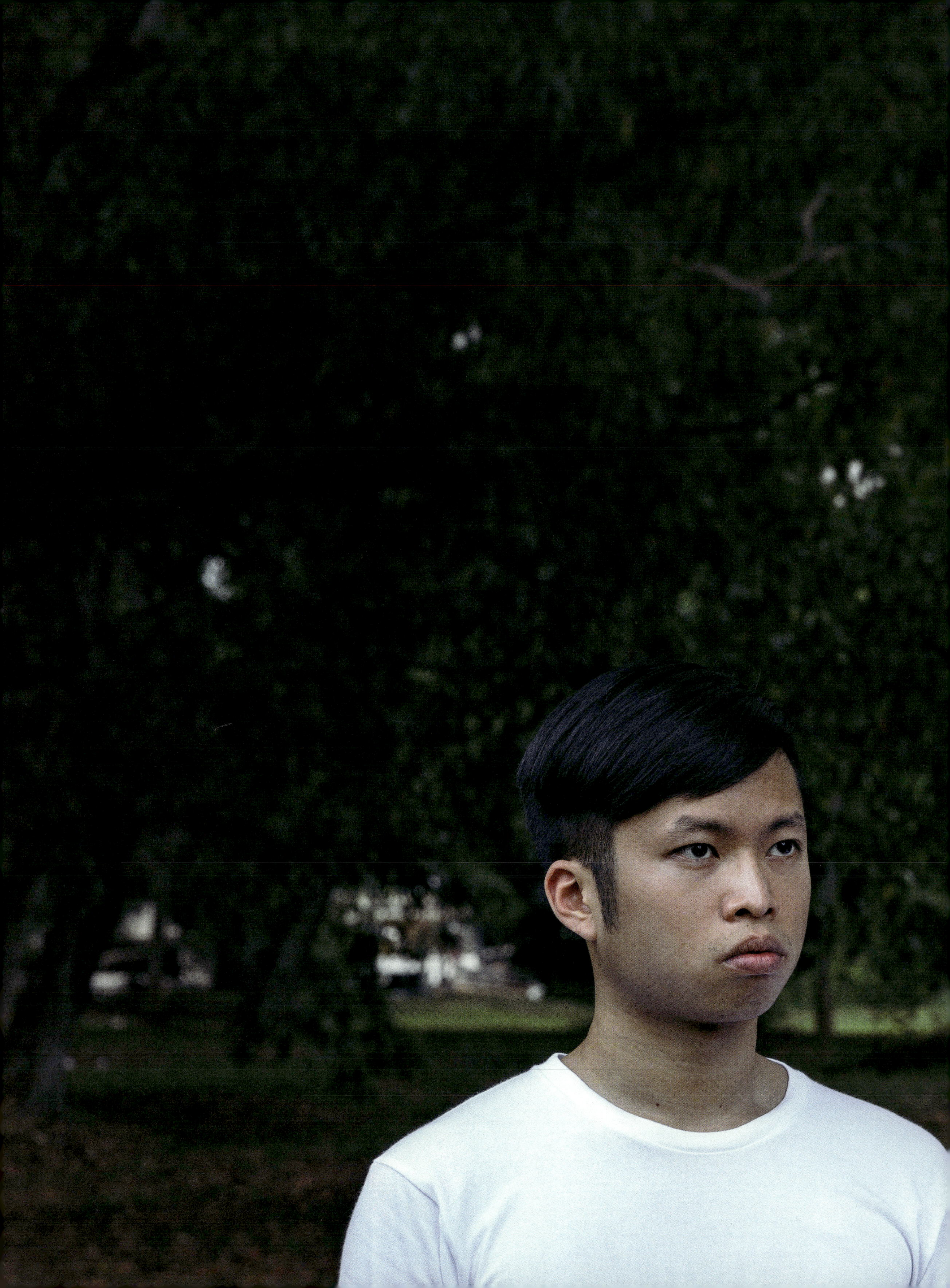

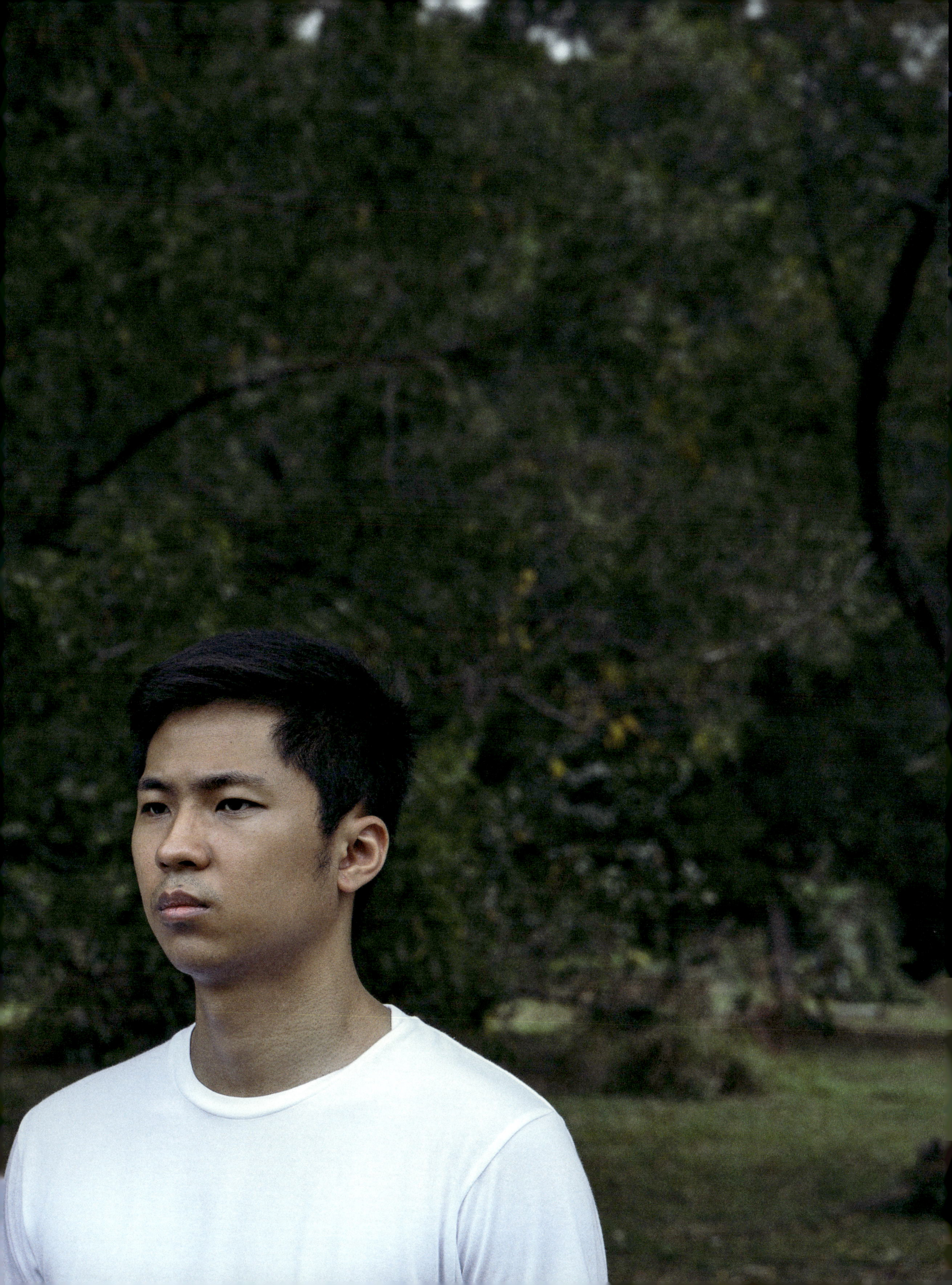

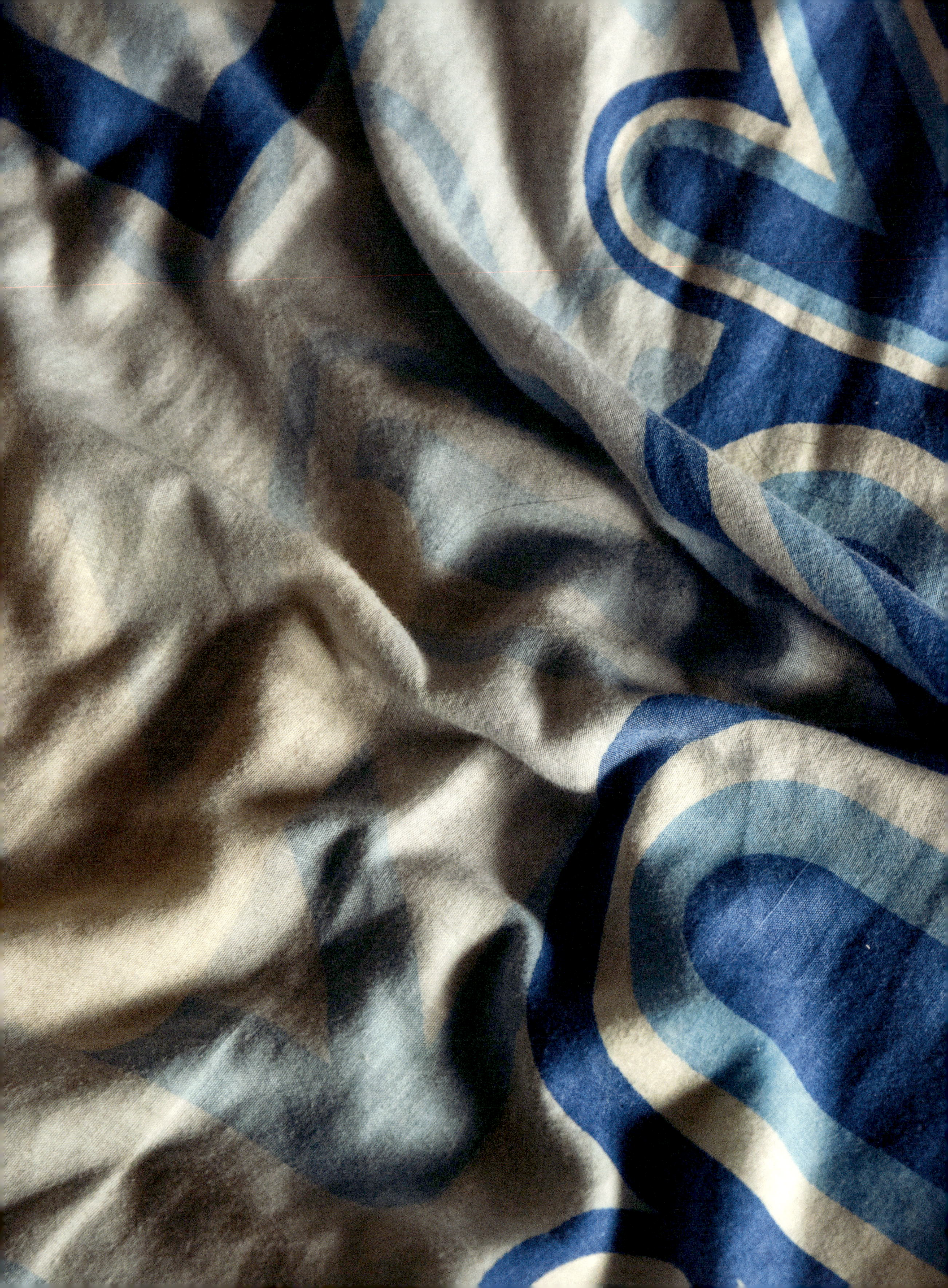

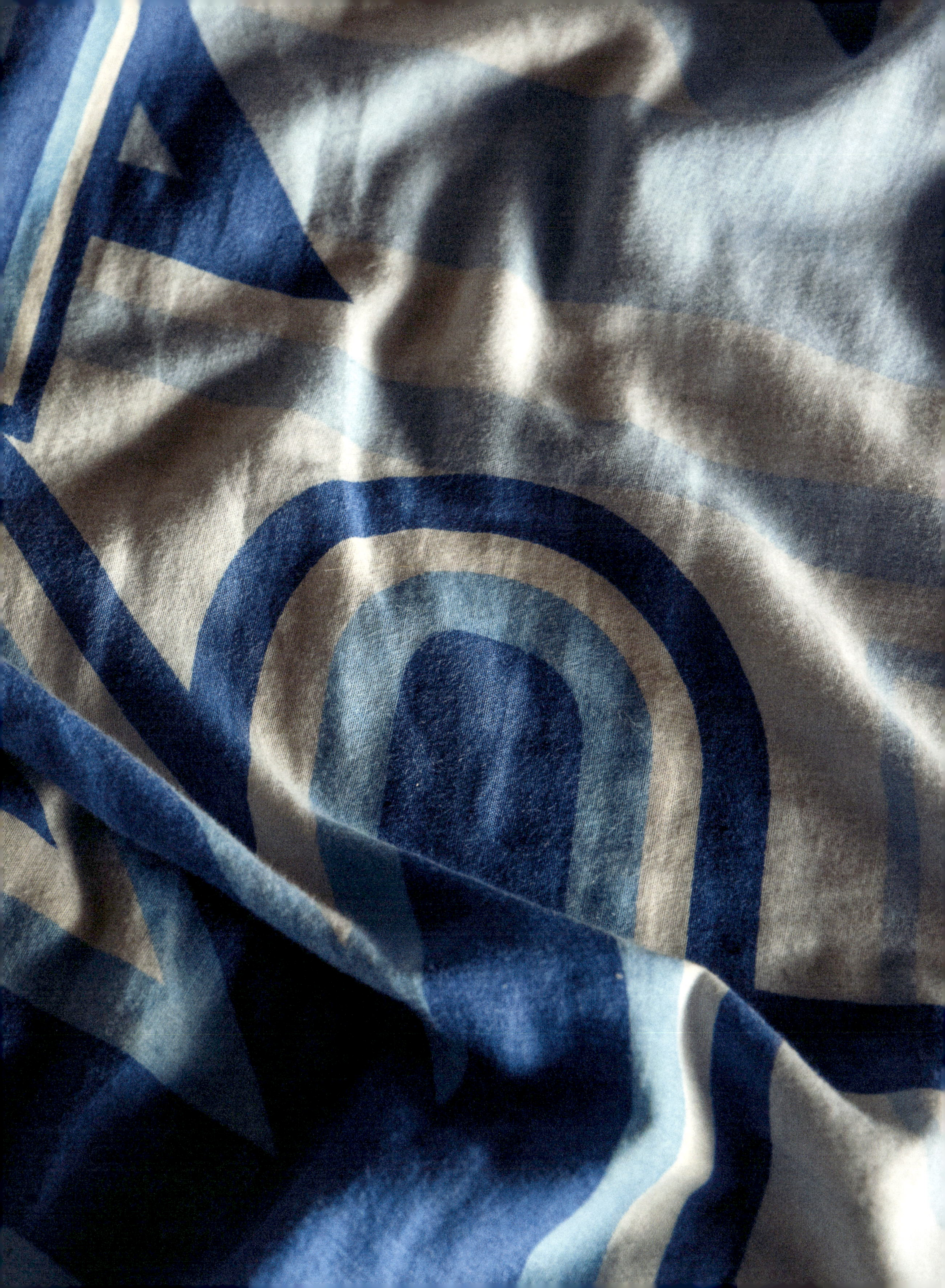

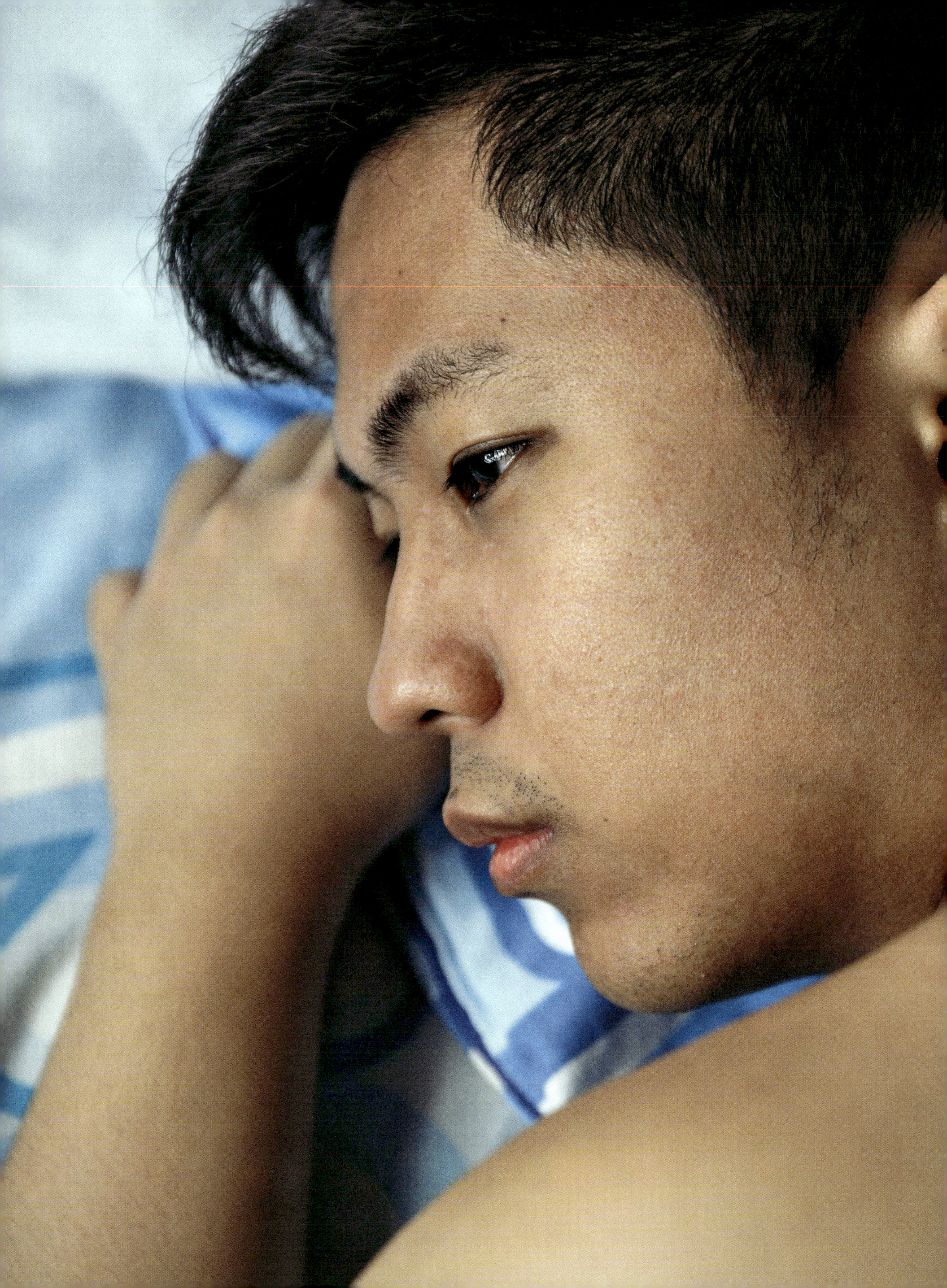

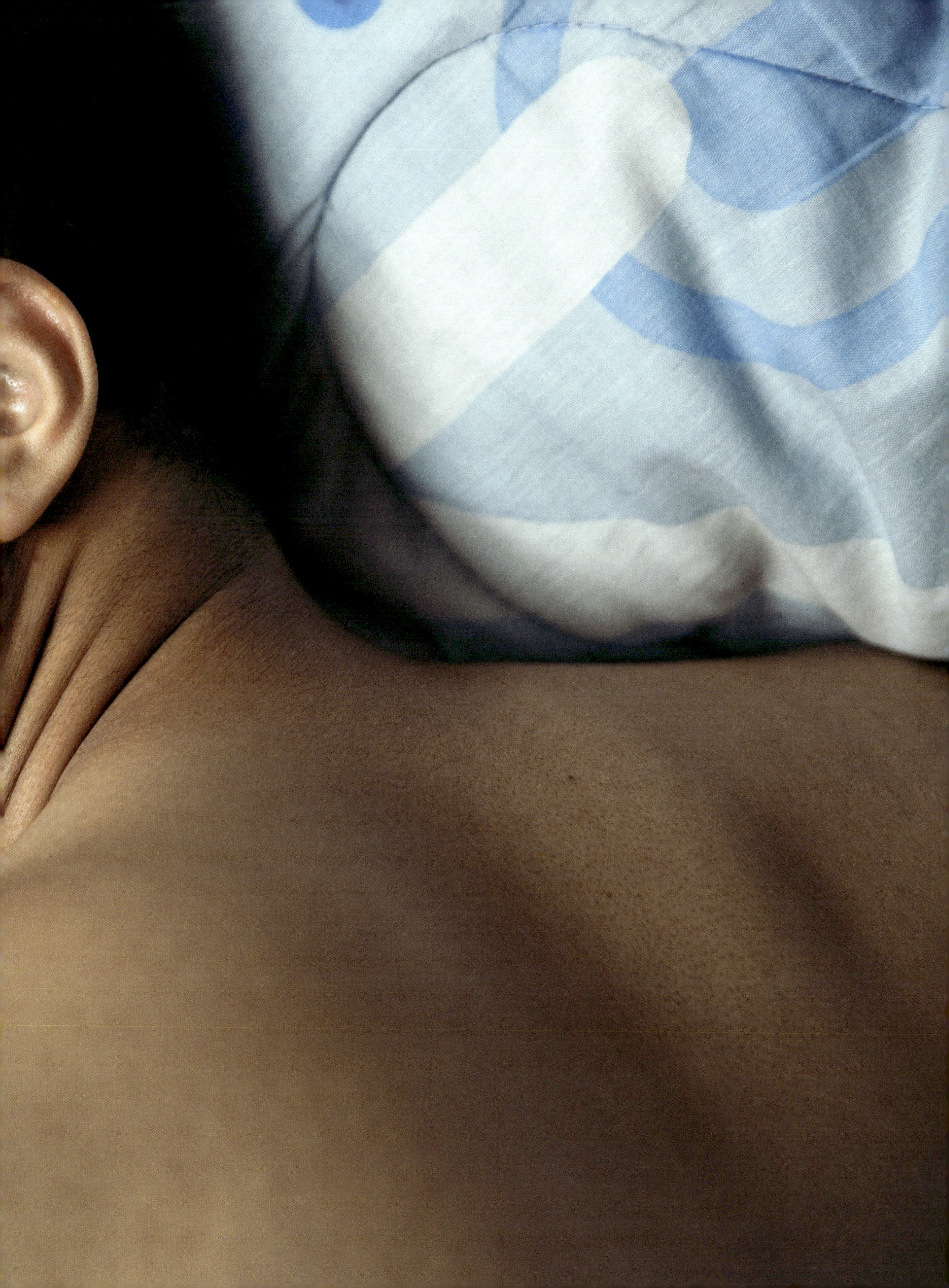

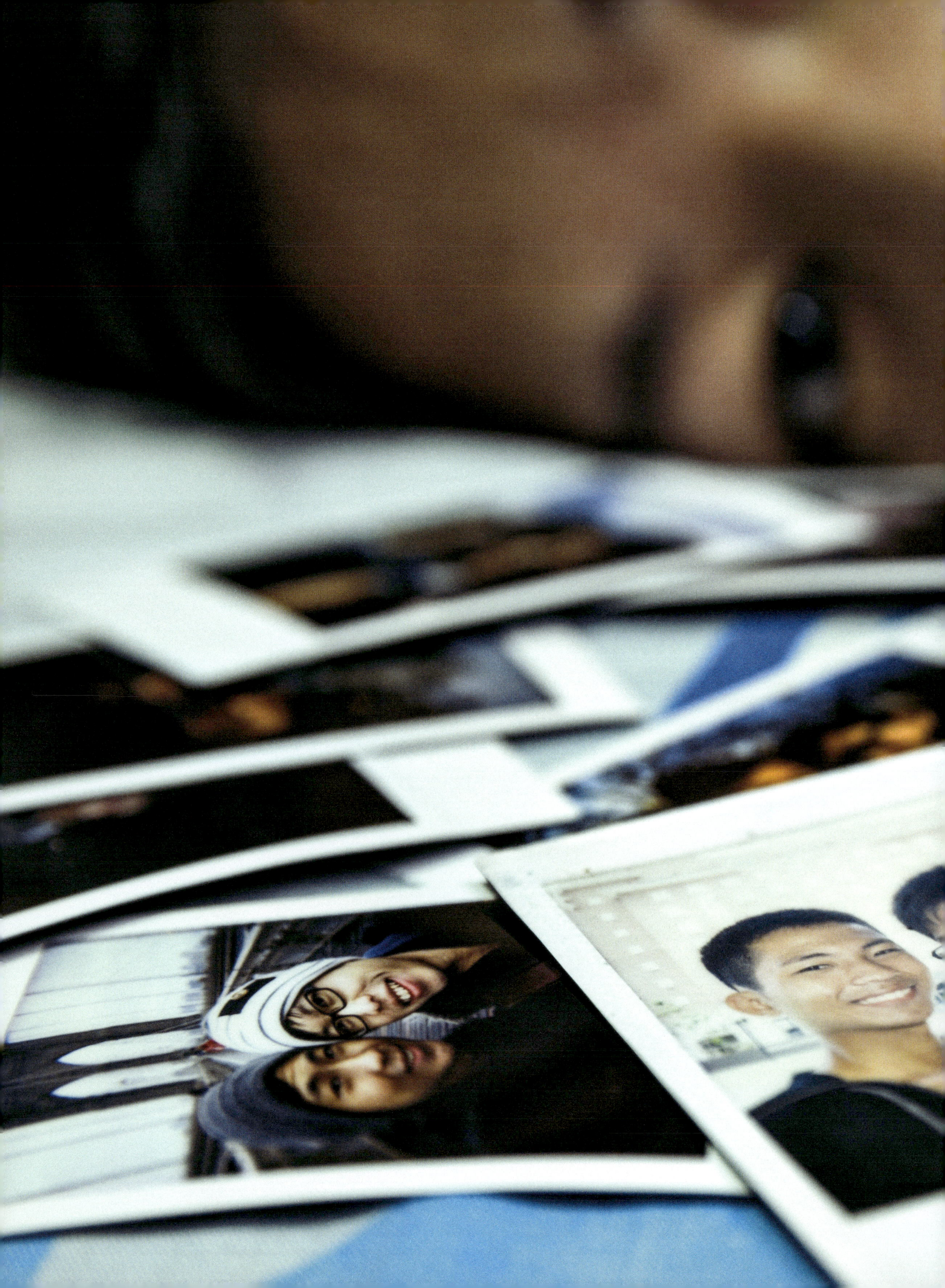

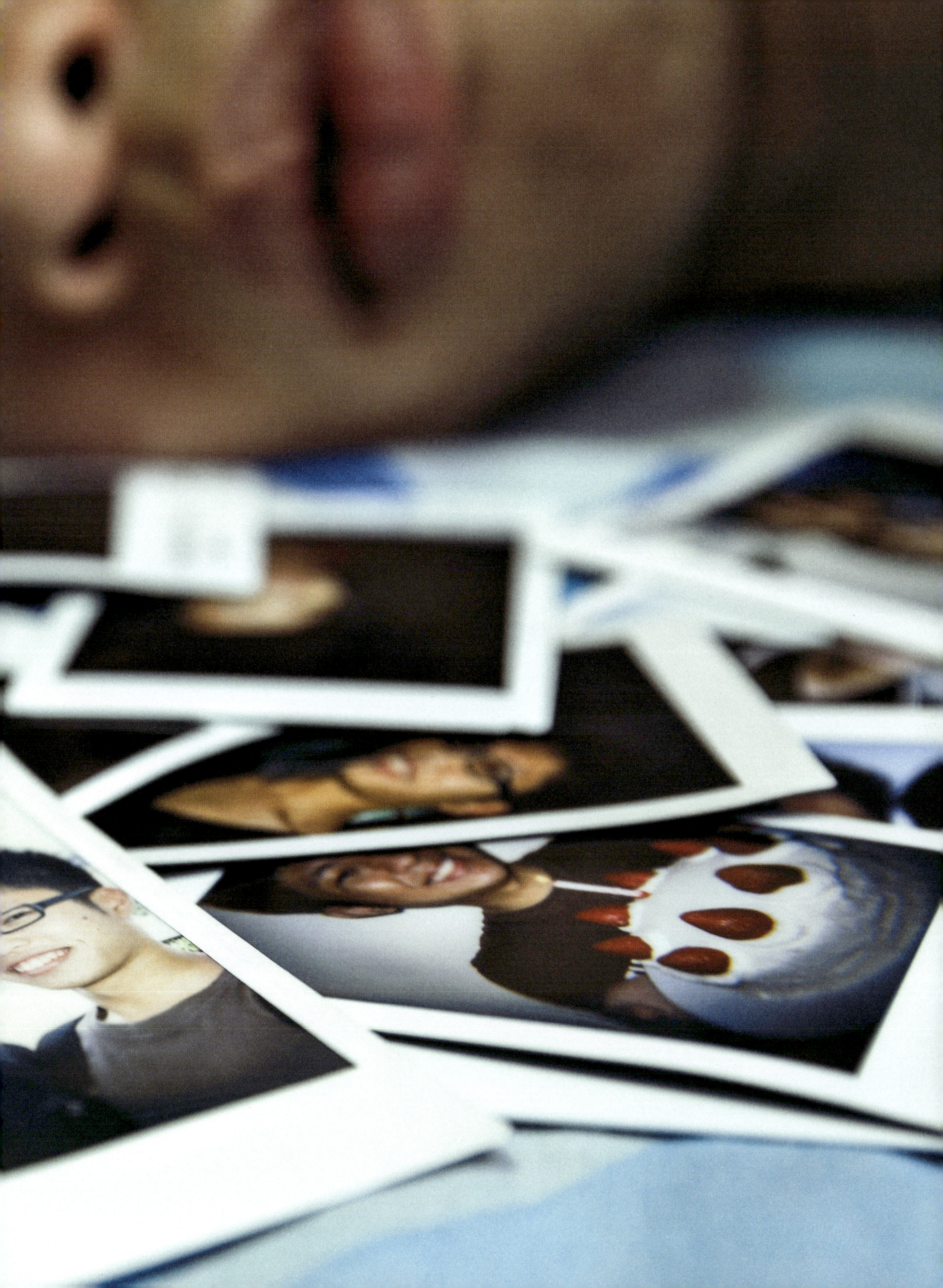

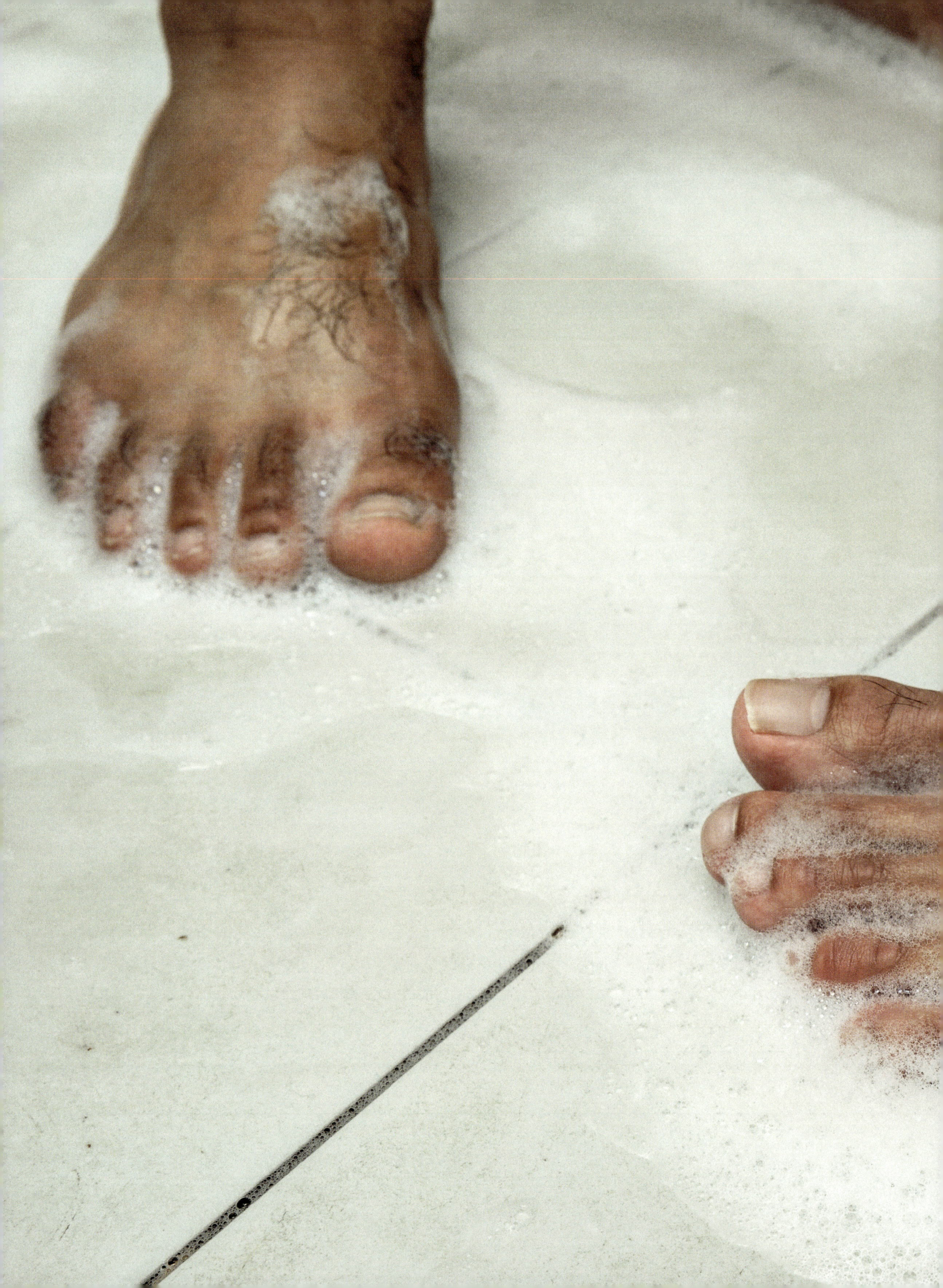

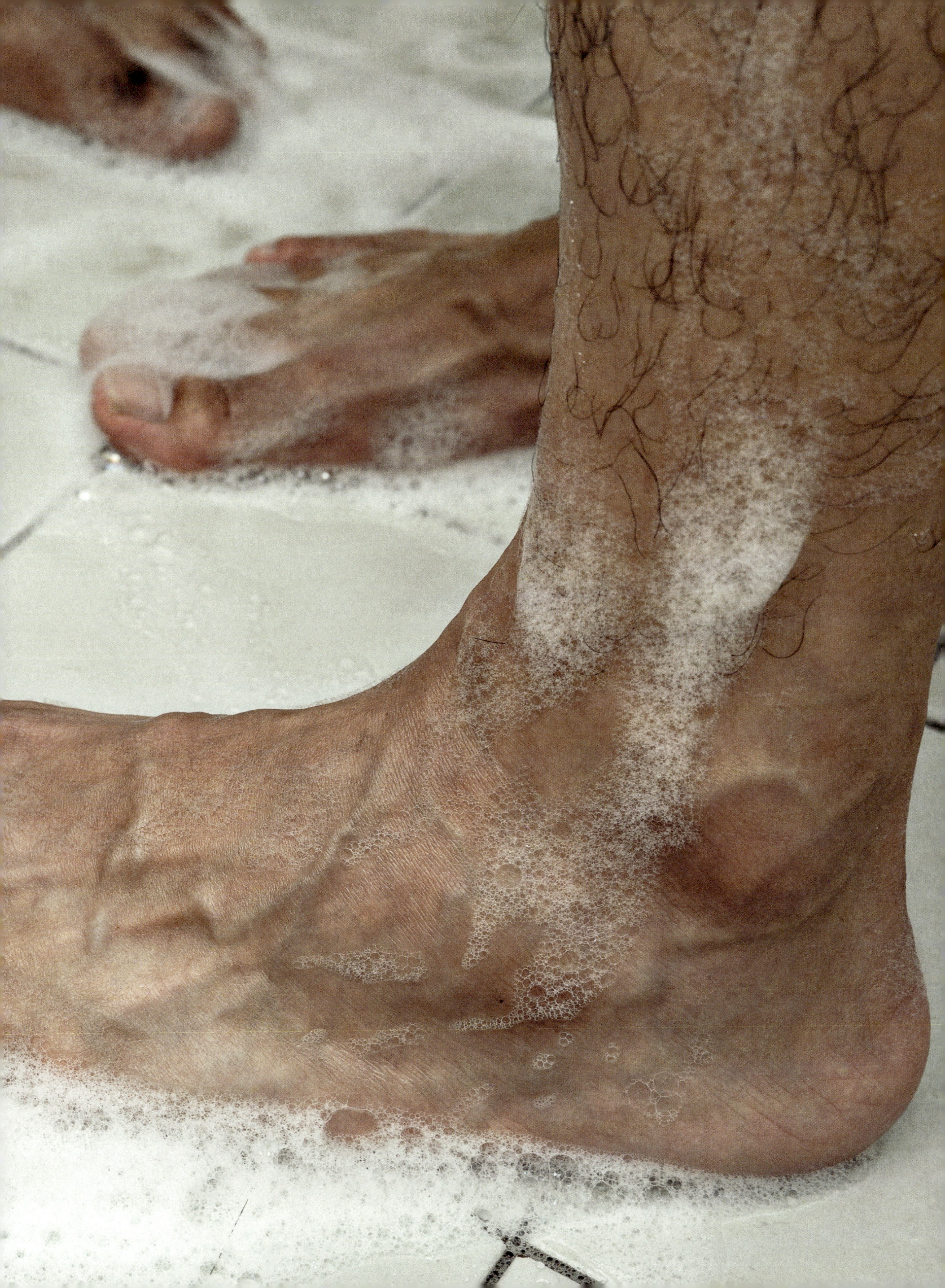

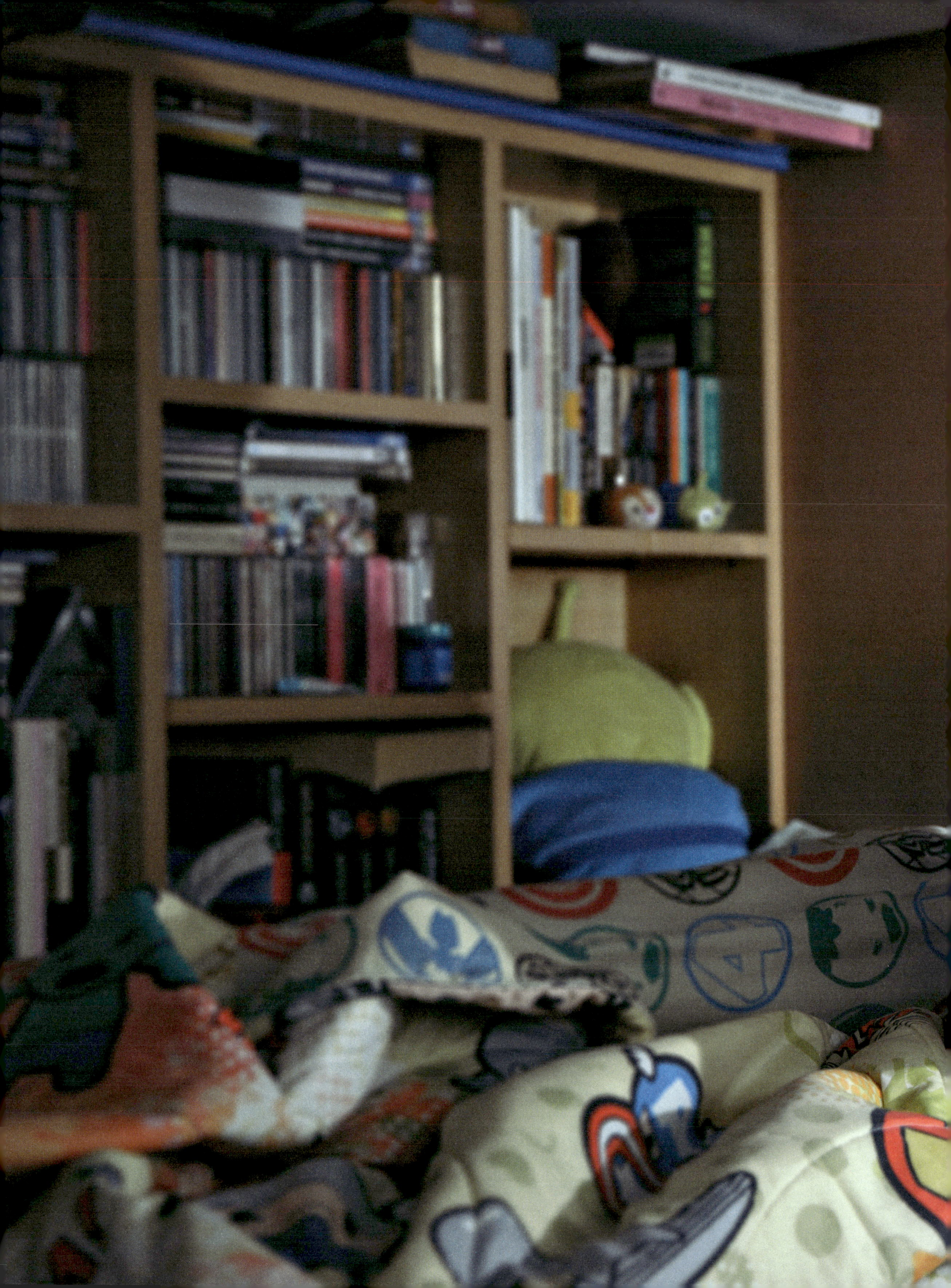

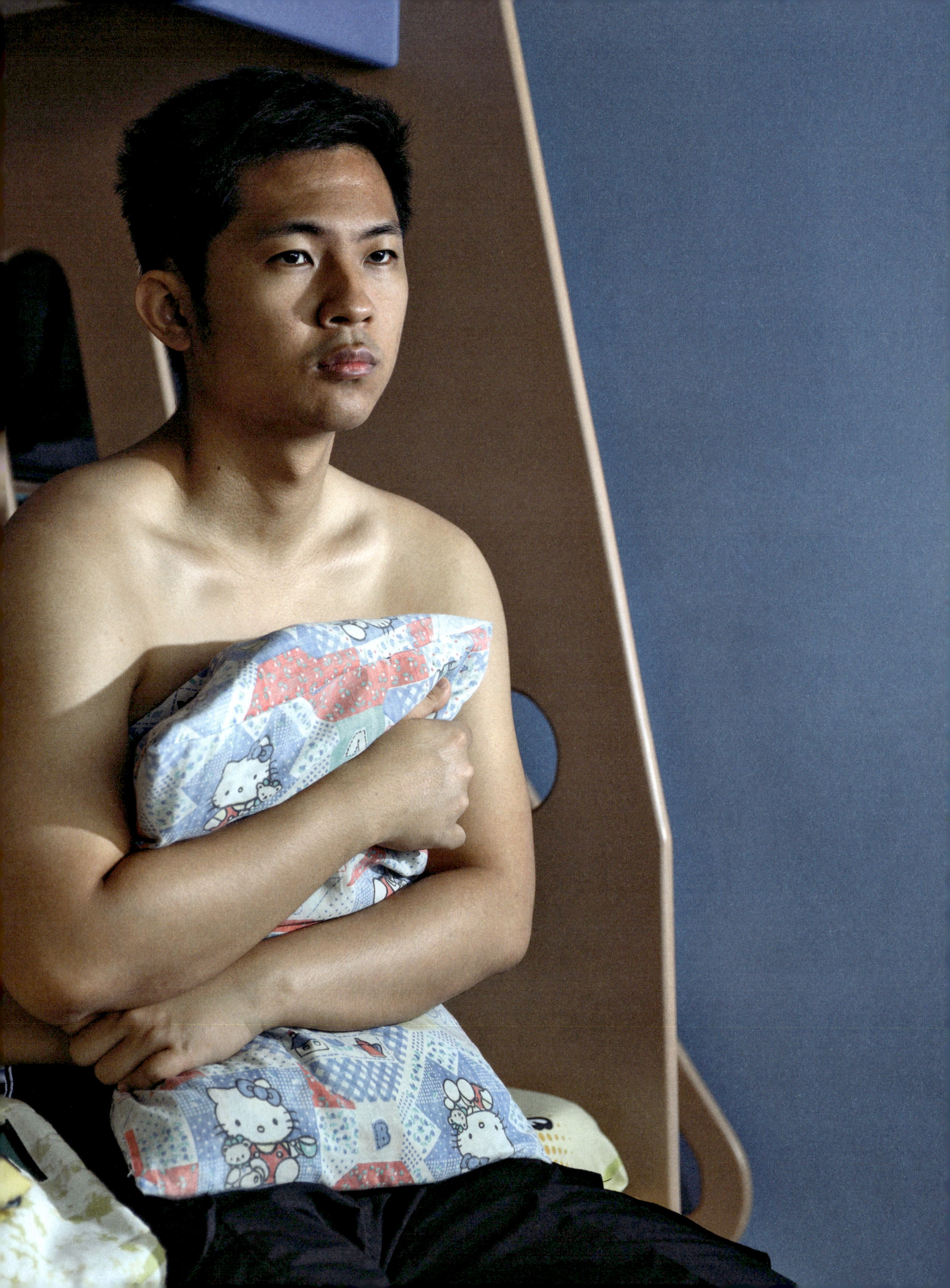

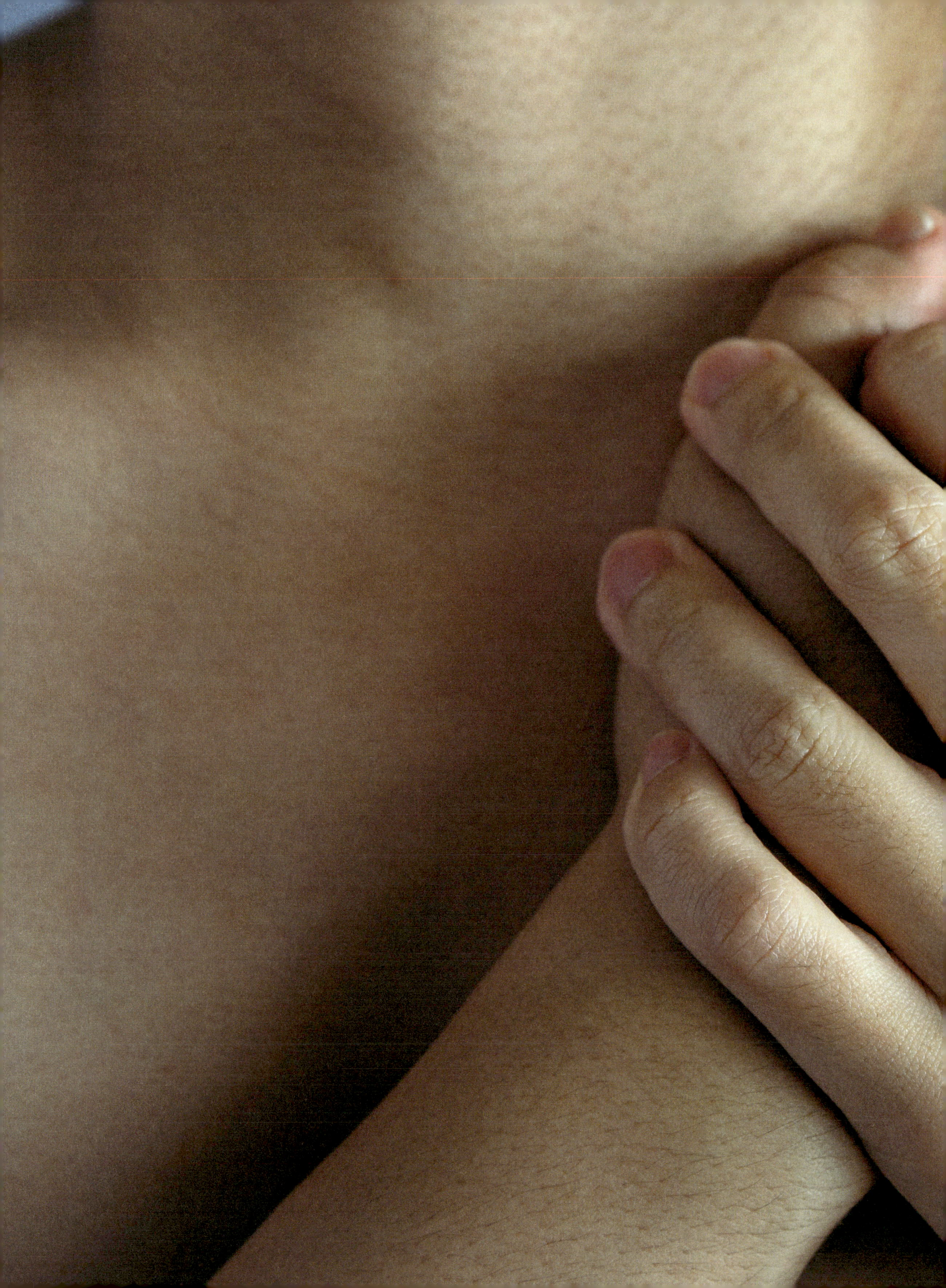

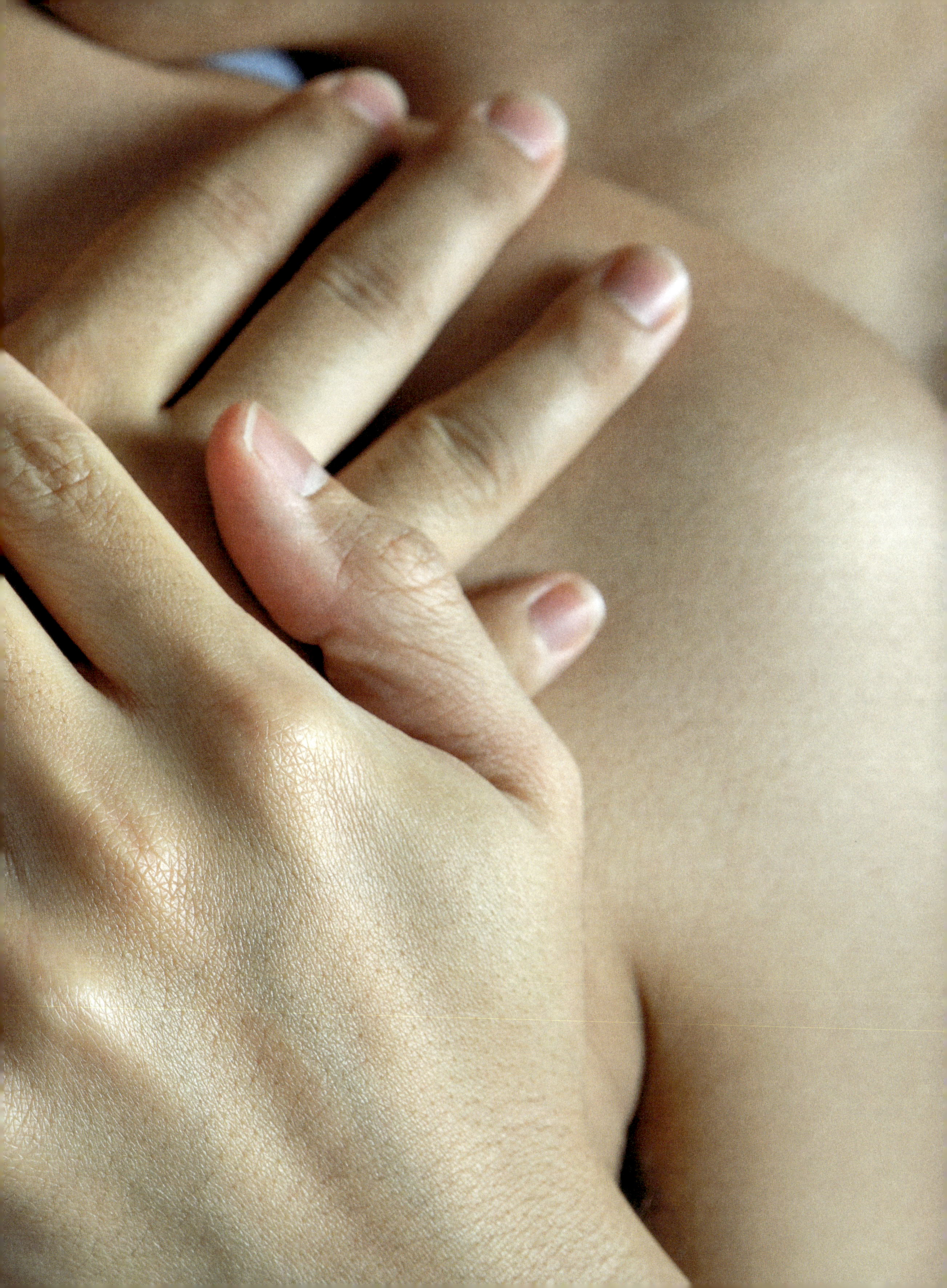

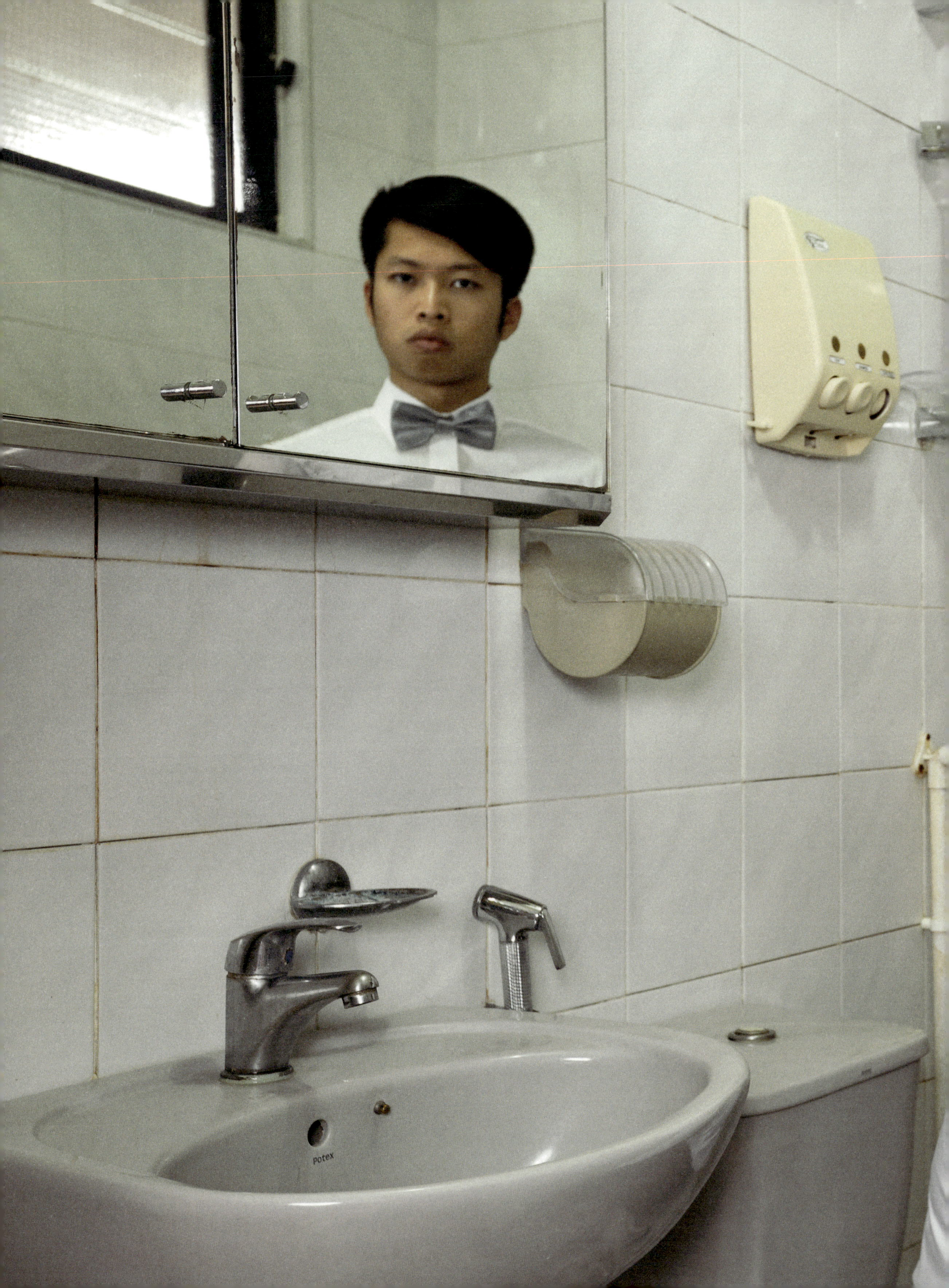

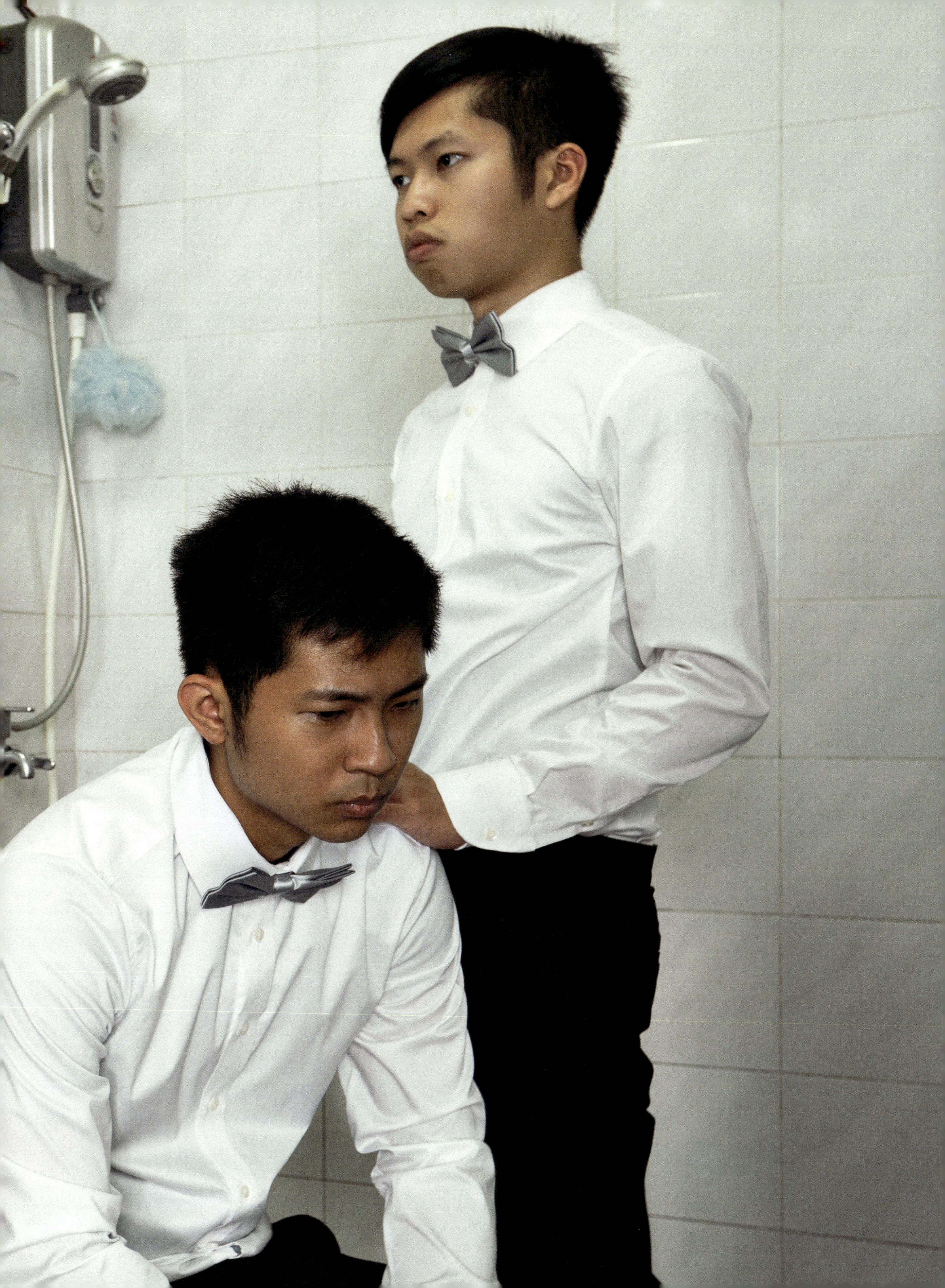

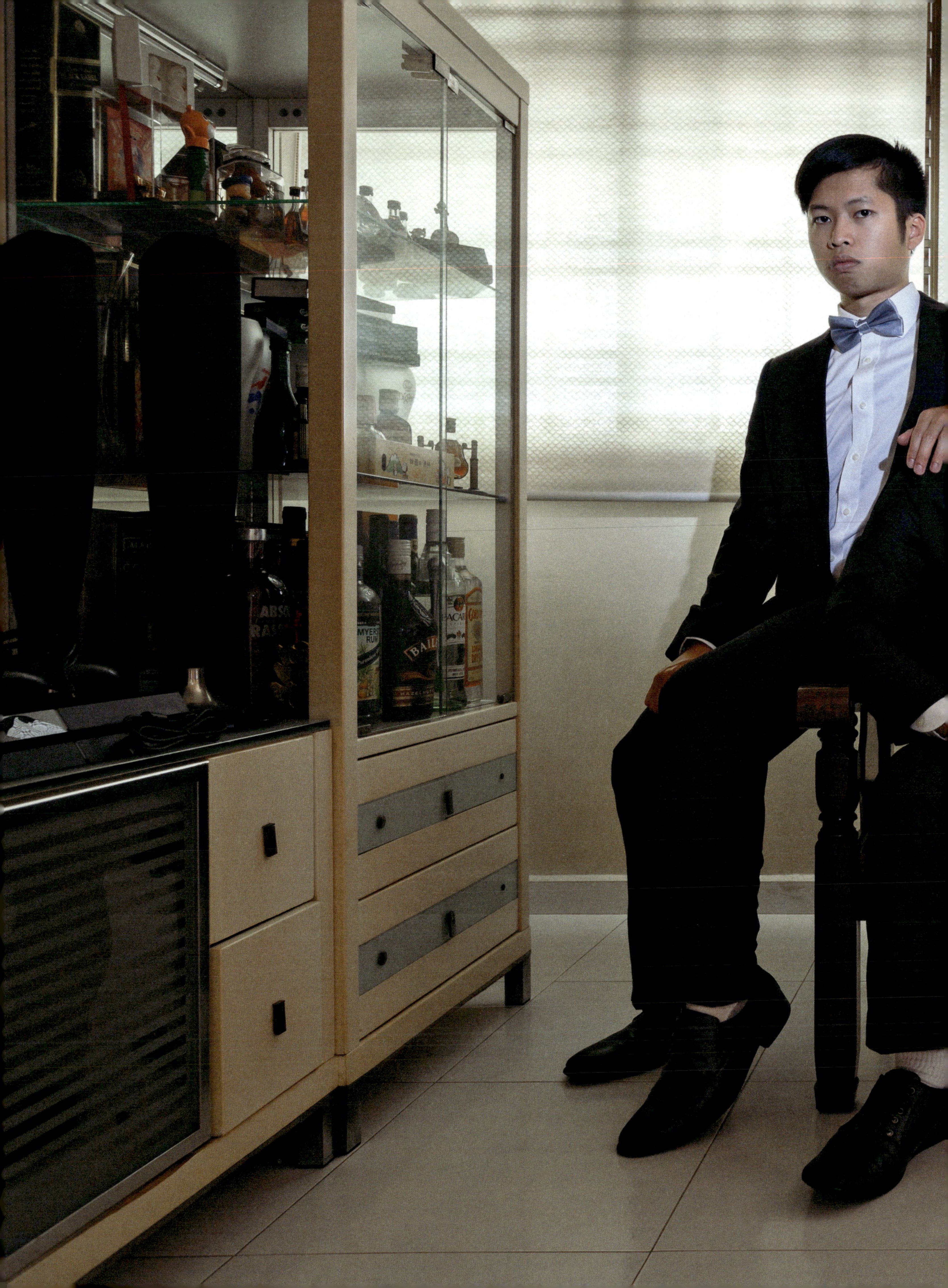

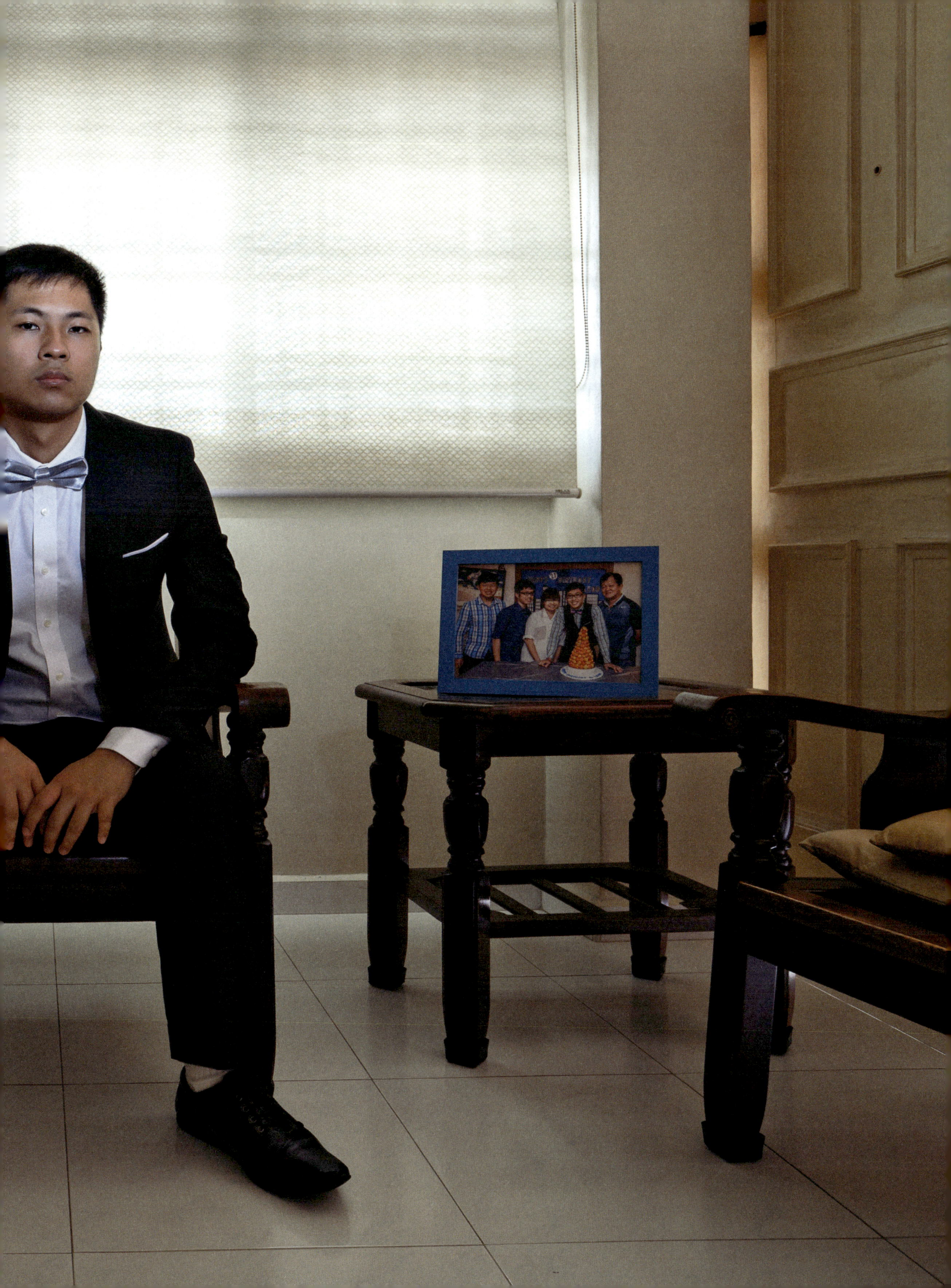

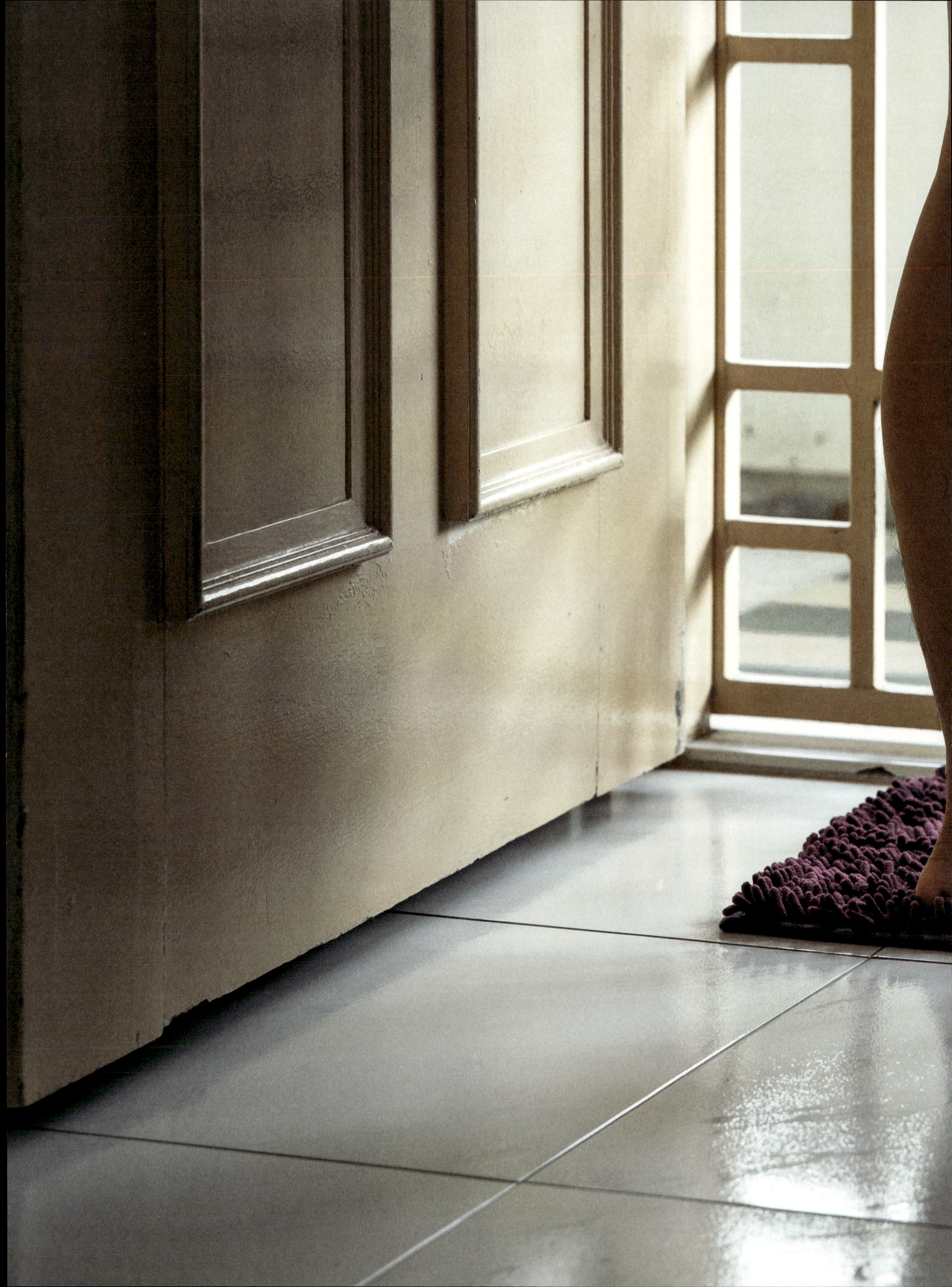

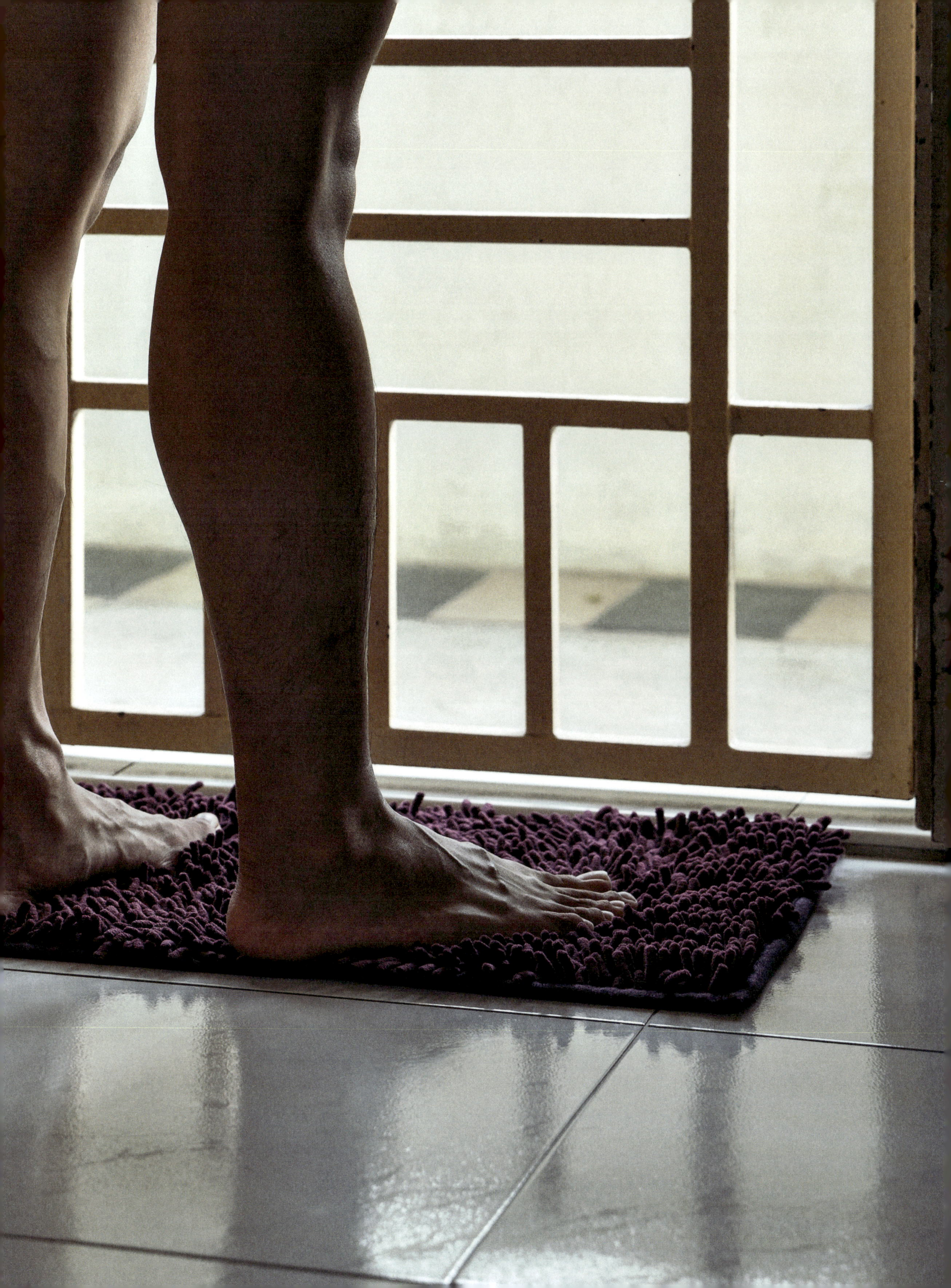

uncertainty in our strides,
we step out of our imaginary hell
into yet another purgatory
of this cruel world

How will they speak
of our childish acts?
But we are all merely children,
awaiting Judgment.

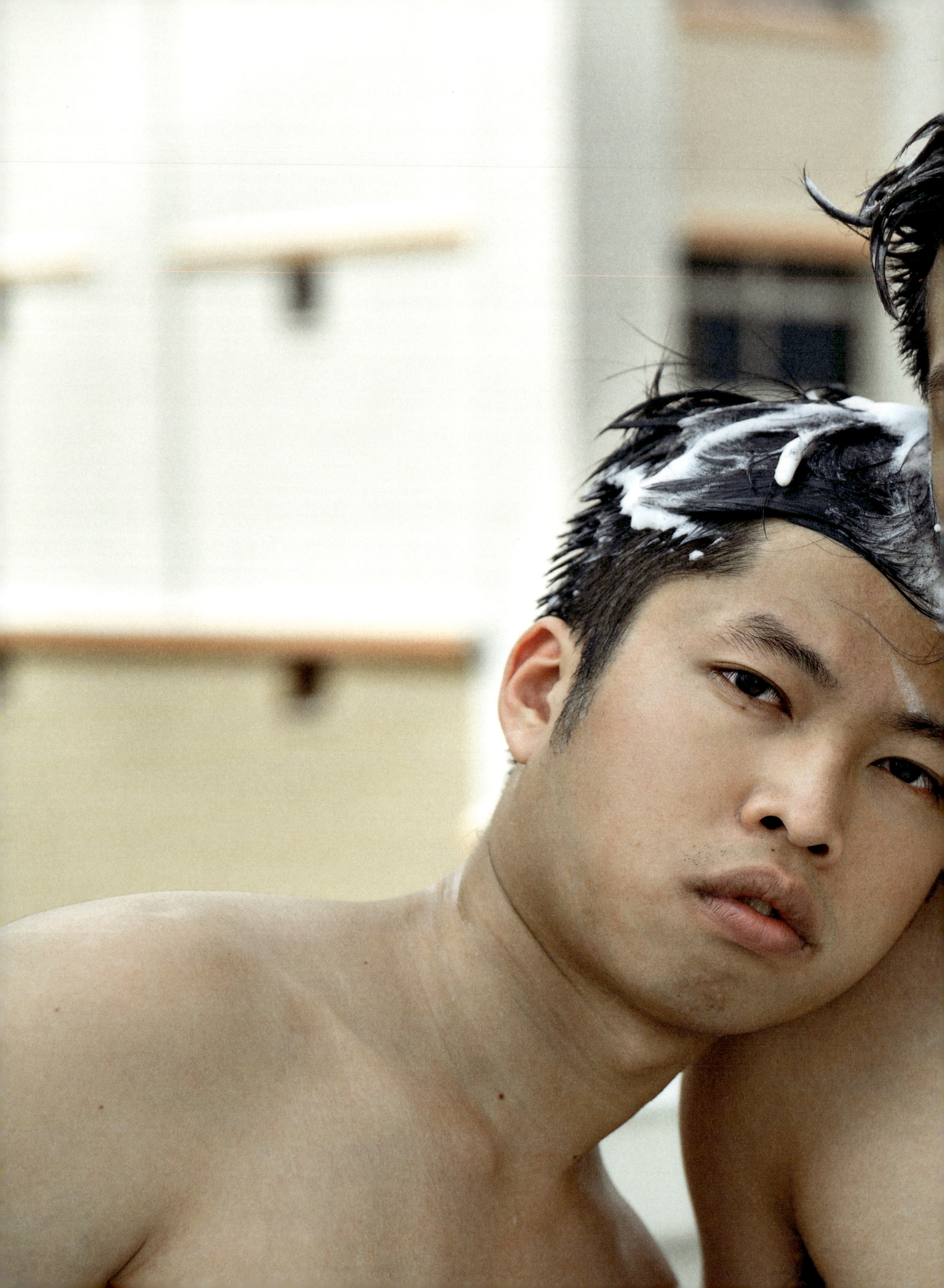

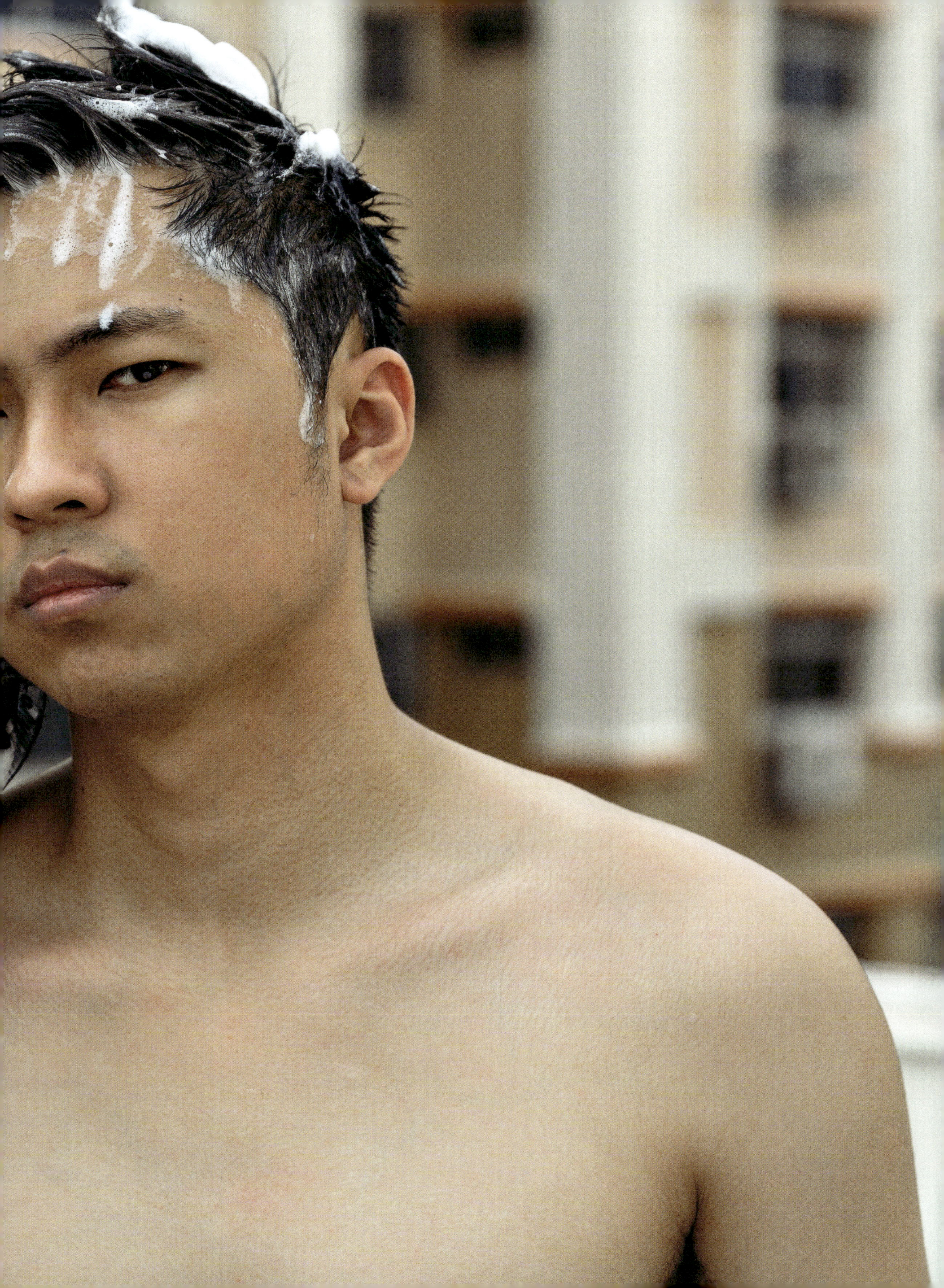

For now, we are free
Even if it were short lived,
at least we lived.

Even if we fall from the skies, burning
at least we lived.

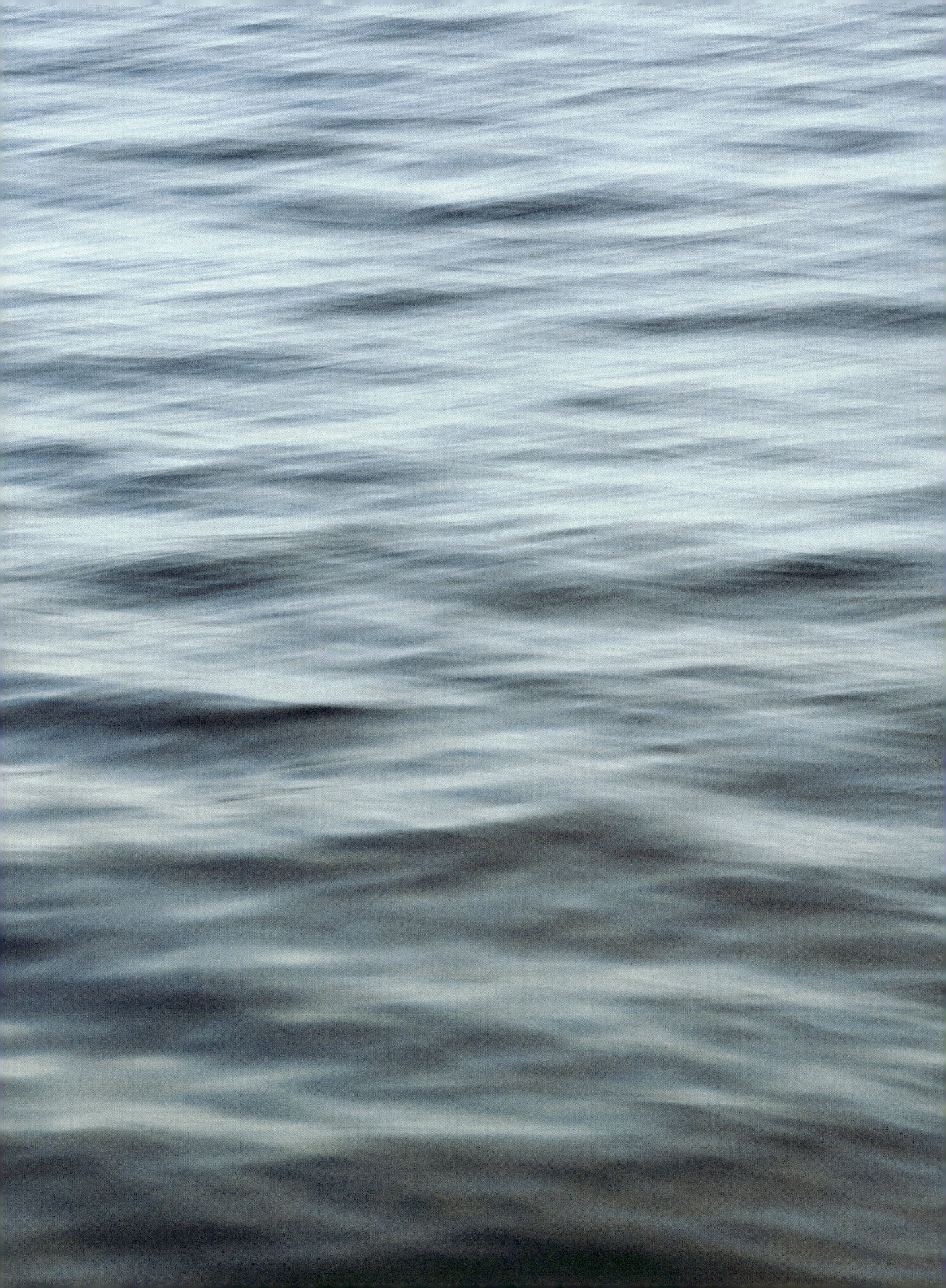

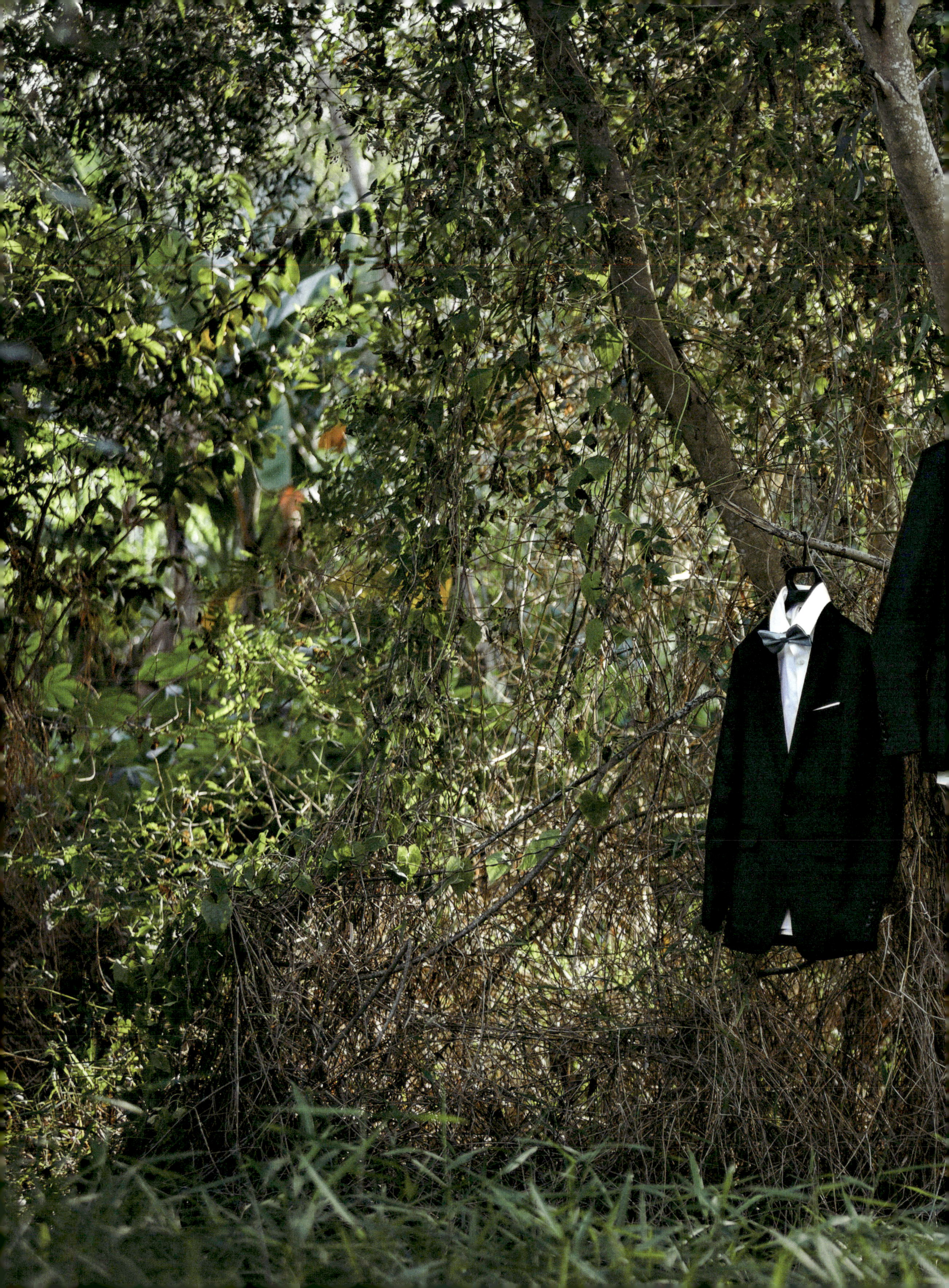

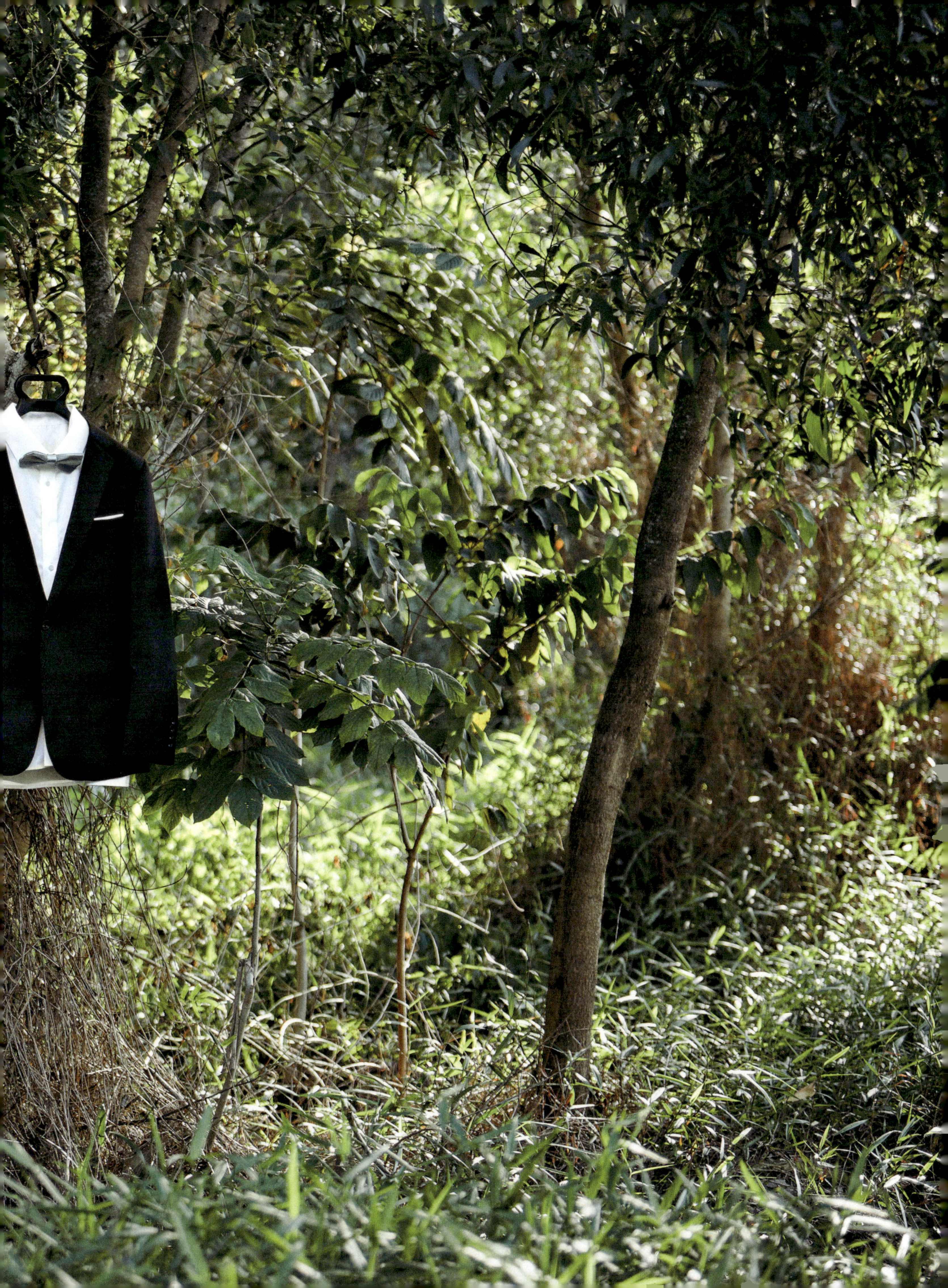

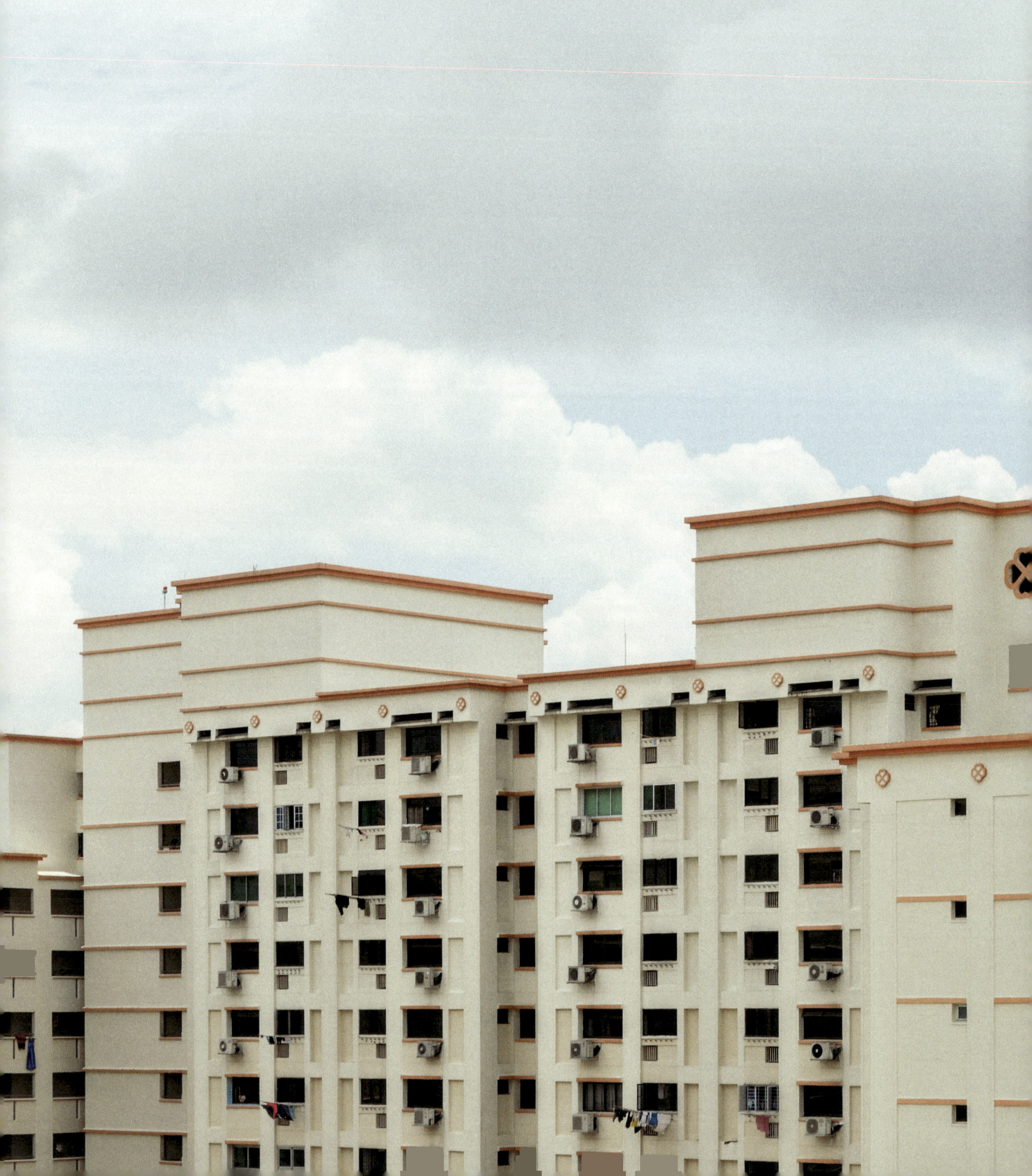

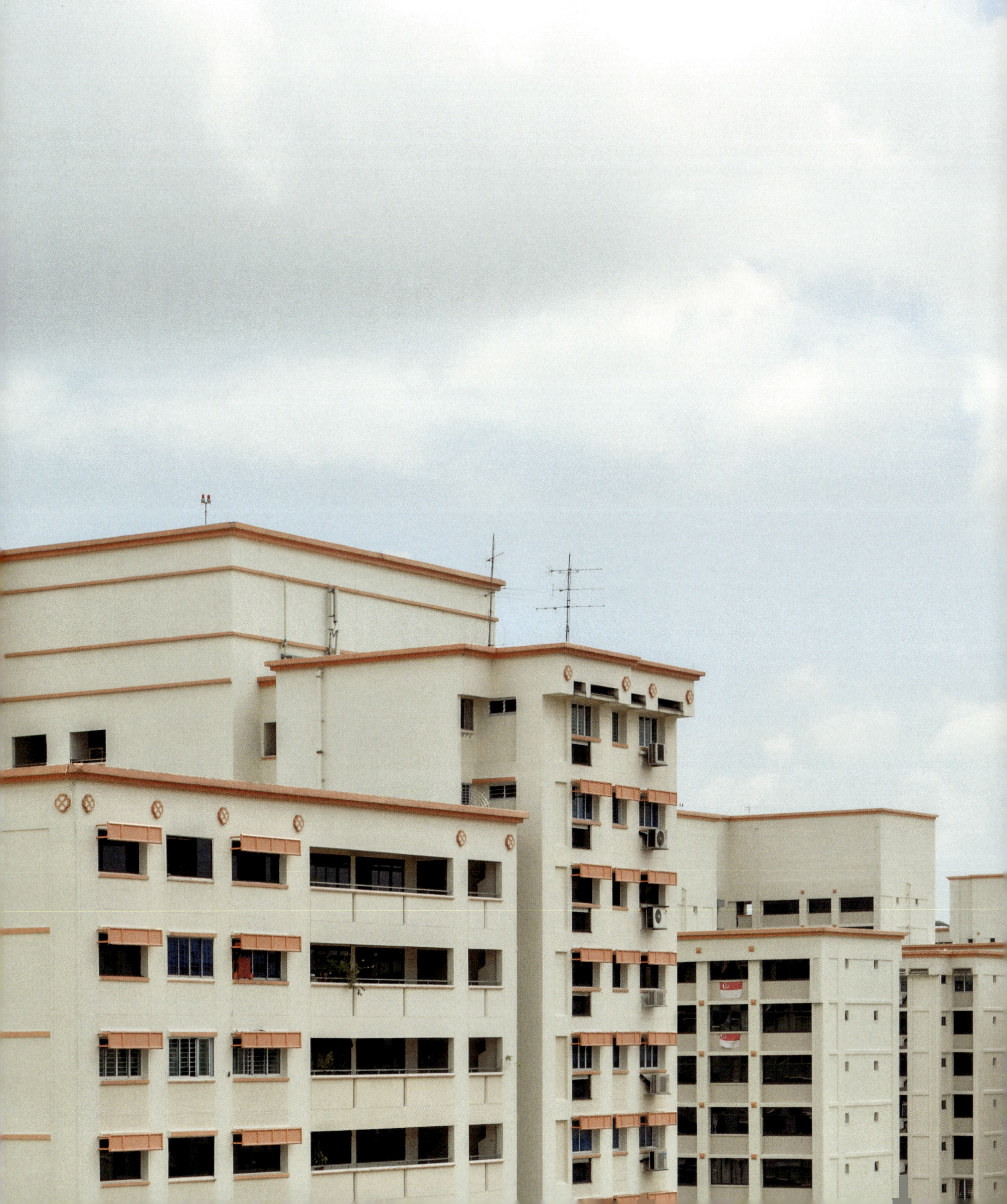

“你吃饱了吗？”

Steidl Book Award Asia

In the spring of 2016 the exhibition "1001 Steidl Books" was held at DECK in Singapore, an independent platform for art and photography. On the occasion of the exhibition artists from across Asia were invited to submit book dummies for the Steidl Book Award Asia. A single award was planned, but from the many books Gerhard Steidl finally chose eight: "The submissions were all so strong, so surprising and varied, that it would have been unfair to just choose one." Together with the founder and director of DECK Gwen Lee, and the creative director of WERK Theseus Chan, the eight photographers came to Steidl in Göttingen in January 2017 and made their books.

The award winners are:

Yukari Chikura, *Zaido* (Japan)
ISBN 978-3-95829-313-7

Kapil Das, *Something So Clear* (India)
ISBN 978-3-95829-318-2

Zhang Lijie, *Midnight Tweedle* (China)
ISBN 978-3-95829-314-4

Broy Lim, *and now they know* (Singapore)
ISBN 978-3-95829-312-0

Jongwoo Park, *DMZ: Demilitarized Zone of Korea* (South Korea)
ISBN 978-3-95829-315-1

Robert Zhao Renhui, *A Guide to the Flora and Fauna of the World* (Singapore)
ISBN 978-3-95829-319-9

Woong Soak Teng, *Ways to Tie Trees* (Singapore)
ISBN 978-3-95829-316-8

Jake Verzosa, *The Last Tattooed Women of Kalinga* (Philippines)
ISBN 978-3-95829-317-5

For further information visit steidl.de

First edition published in 2017

Book design: Broy Lim, Theseus Chan
Color separations by Steidl's digital darkroom

Production and printing: Steidl, Göttingen

Steidl
Düstere Str. 4 / 37073 Göttingen, Germany
Phone +49 551 49 60 60 / Fax +49 551 49 60 649
mail@steidl.de
steidl.de

ISBN 978-3-95829-312-0
Printed in Germany by Steidl